"We are not defined by what we do for God, we are defined by what God already did for us! My pastor and friend, Robert Morris, presents the biblically substantiated case that at the end of the day it is all about the grace of Jesus, period. When we embrace the grace of Christ, we can then fill the earth with the glory of God. This is a definitive must-read, must-do, must-share, must-live!"

—Rev. Samuel Rodriguez, New Season lead pastor, NHCLC president/CEO, author of *Your Mess, God's Miracle*, and executive producer of *Breakthrough* and *Flamin' Hot*

"The amazing grace of God is often misunderstood, overlooked, or misapplied. In *Grace, Period. Living in the Amazing Reality of Jesus' Finished Work*, Robert not only unlocks the beauty and perfection of God's grace, but shows us how to live the abundant life that Jesus came to give us. This book will help every Believer to live in freedom and to flourish in life."

—Christine Caine, founder of A21 and Propel Women

"One of the most loved hymns is entitled 'Amazing Grace,' and yet how many have sung this song and failed to truly grasp what is so amazing about Grace? In this book, Pastor Robert takes you on a journey, where he leads you and invites you to meet grace face-to-face, to see grace in all its fullness, so that it will no longer be a lyric you merely sing, but a reality you passionately embrace. You will see just how sweet the sound is…of the grace you are."

—Charlotte Gambil, international speaker and author

"God's grace is the one thing that sets us free from our fears and burdens—even our self-imposed burdens. And there's no one better to describe the joys of that freedom in every intricate, beautiful detail than Robert Morris."

—John C. Maxwell, *New York Times* bestselling author, executive coach, pastor, and speaker who has sold more than 37 million books in 50 languages

"Clear and compelling. Challenging and fortifying. In *Grace, Period.*, Pastor Robert provides a roadmap to overcome the tyranny of shame and striving and discover the abundant life God sent Jesus to die for. The grace that gets us to heaven is the same grace that gets us to the end of the week—and this book does a masterful job of helping readers discover that grace."

—Louie Giglio, pastor of Passion City Church, founder of Passion Conferences, author of *Don't Give the Enemy a Seat at Your Table*

"This book is filled with practical teaching and so many wonderful personal stories that will help you understand God's grace in a whole new way and truly receive it for your life."

—Joyce Meyer, Bible teacher and bestselling author

"Pastor Morris's book shakes up everything we've thought about grace. His definition of the word expands and reiterates what it means to receive God's gift of grace for all believers."

—Nick Vujicic, founder of Life Without Limbs, servant of the Most High

"We need to understand that grace is more than a concept...It fuels life and is a truth that we need deeply embedded in all aspects of our lives. Thank you Pastor Robert for reminding us of that!"

—Dr. Henry Cloud, psychologist and *New York Times* bestselling author

"May God bless this book and all who read it with a fresh sense of His great grace."   —Max Lucado, pastor and author

"I'm so glad that my dear friend, Pastor Robert Morris, has taken the time to carefully explore the many facets of grace and to expound on its wonder!"

—John Bevere, bestselling author and minister, co-founder of Messenger International and MessengerX

GRACE, PERIOD.

Also by Robert Morris

Beyond Blessed: God's Perfect Plan to Overcome
All Financial Stress

Daily Readings from Beyond Blessed

Take the Day Off: Receiving God's Gift of Rest

Seven Words of Christmas: The Joyful Prophecies
That Changed the World

GRACE, PERIOD.

Living in the Amazing Reality of
Jesus' Finished Work

ROBERT MORRIS

FaithWords

NASHVILLE   NEW YORK

FaithWords
Hachette Book Group
1290 Avenue of the Americas, New York, NY 10104
faithwords.com
twitter.com/faithwords

First Edition: April 2024

FaithWords is a division of Hachette Book Group, Inc. The FaithWords name and logo are trademarks of Hachette Book Group, Inc.

The publisher is not responsible for websites (or their content) that are not owned by the publisher.

The Hachette Speakers Bureau provides a wide range of authors for speaking events. To find out more, go to hachettespeakersbureau.com or email HachetteSpeakers@hbgusa.com.

FaithWords books may be purchased in bulk for business, educational, or promotional use. For information, please contact your local bookseller or the Hachette Book Group Special Markets Department at special.markets@hbgusa.com.

Additional credit information is on page 239.

Library of Congress Cataloging-in-Publication Data
Names: Morris, Robert (Robert Preston), 1961- author.
Title: Grace, period : living in the amazing reality of Jesus' finished work / Robert Morris.
Description: First edition. | Nashville : FaithWords, 2024. | Includes bibliographical references.
Identifiers: LCCN 2023041042 | ISBN 9781546004936 (hardcover) | ISBN 9781546004967 (ebook)
Subjects: LCSH: Grace (Theology) | Salvation—Christianity.
Classification: LCC BT761.3 .M667 2024 | DDC 234—dc23/eng/20231127
LC record available at https://lccn.loc.gov/2023041042

ISBNs: 9781546004936 (hardcover), 9781546004967 (ebook)

Printed in the United States of America

LSC-C

Printing 1, 2024

CONTENTS

CONTENTS

START HERE

It's Grace... Period.

The meeting began with surprise and unbridled joy, but suddenly it took a hard left turn without signaling, veering off into strange territory. In a matter of minutes, we'd moved from mutual delight to awkwardness. Something I had eagerly looked forward to—something precious and holy to me—had suddenly been tainted. Allow me to back up a few steps and explain what rapidly turned my joy into disappointment that day.

Roughly twenty-two years ago, as a (relatively) young pastor of a young church, I saw my very first book published. At the time, I could not have dreamed how God would use *The Blessed Life* to help, encourage, and inspire people. God breathed on my humble offering as only He can. In the beginning, we self-published the book after some encouragement from longtime friend James Robison. When James introduced his sizable *Life Today* television audience to *The Blessed Life*, the entire first run of thirty thousand books was snapped up. A second printing, and then a third soon followed. Eventually the book was picked up by a mainstream publisher, and many hundreds of thousands of additional copies found their way into the hands of believers all over the world. In the years since, additional versions from various sources and varying formats have found their way into print. After more than two decades, I continue to marvel that, year after year, it still finds its way into the hands of believers in large numbers.

I wrote *The Blessed Life* with one aim—to help God's people discover the sheer wondrous, hilarious joy of generosity. Not "giving to get," but rather giving from a pure heart of gratitude for salvation in Jesus. Giving because we're never more like our heavenly Father when we do so. Giving because we're free to be generous in the liberating assurance that we simply can't outgive God. Into that book I poured not theory or mere theology but real, lived experience with God. I built it on the testimony of what my wife, Debbie, and I personally witnessed on our lifelong adventure of imitating our wildly generous God.

Yes, there was lots of Bible in *The Blessed Life*, but what captured the imaginations of so many were our true stories. Stories of the times we emptied our bank accounts in order to follow a prompting of the Holy Spirit to help someone. Stories of the times we gave away paid-for cars. And even a house! We told these stories not to boast but to testify. It was God who gave us a revelation of generosity and a heart to give. And it was God who demonstrated His faithfulness to not only meet our needs but also bless us extravagantly when we did so. Which brings me to that meeting I mentioned in the opening sentence.

Years ago, Debbie and I knew a woman who had been struggling in many areas of her life, including her finances. I clearly heard the Holy Spirit say He wanted to bless her with a significant gift of money. I checked with Debbie and she wholeheartedly agreed. As we set up a time to meet with this woman to deliver the gift, we were excited to once again be a part of demonstrating God's love and care to one of His beloved children. When you hold everything God has entrusted to you with an open hand and keep the ears of your spirit open to prompts from the Holy Spirit, you find you get many opportunities to bless others. You don't do it to be thanked. You do it because you are God's child, and a child naturally takes after his or her father. You do it because God loves people, and delights in using us to let them know they're seen and treasured by Him.

When we met with this precious woman and handed over the blessing, she was at first stunned and speechless. Her confusion, however, quickly melted into tearful rejoicing. And then after a few more minutes, her joy dissolved into...something else.

Her face flushed red as she began stammering about wanting to do something for us in return. She began glancing around the room as if searching for something to give us. We quickly assured her that nothing like that was expected or necessary. We made it as clear as we possibly could that this was a *gift* joyfully given from God, and that we were just the happy delivery folks. Yet she persisted. She then said she would consider the blessing a "loan" and that she would endeavor to pay it back in the days ahead. We did our best to change her thinking but eventually we just prayed for her and left, a little sad, but confident we had done what God had asked us to do.

That woman's failure to simply receive and rejoice was disappointing, but not surprising. I'd seen it before. In fact, it's fairly common. You see, many people simply don't know how to receive a gift. At the root of this is pride. A pride-driven need to feel self-sufficient makes it difficult and sometimes impossible to receive a gift when it is presented.

For countless believers, that trap carries over into their relationship with their heavenly Father. And that's a tragedy. I'll spend the remainder of this book explaining why. You see,

> You see, many people simply don't know how to receive a gift. At the root of this is pride.

grace—in the biblical sense of the word—is inseparable from the concept of gift. In the chapters ahead, you'll discover multiple dimensions of this thing the Bible calls grace.

If you've been a believer for very long at all, you can probably recite the standard textbook definition of *grace*. Most know that grace is unmerited favor from God. And that's not incorrect. It's just inadequate. Woefully inadequate. That two-word cliché does a pitiful disservice to the brilliant, multifaceted jewel of a word that appears 125 times in the New King James Version of the New Testament. It's sort of like defining *peacock* as "a feathered animal." It's not wrong, per se. But it sure doesn't give you much of a sense of what makes a peacock remarkable.

That's why I'm so delighted you've picked up this book. Boy oh boy, do I have good news for you. On the pages ahead, I'm going to take you on a journey of exploration. The territory is called the Land of Grace. Along the way we'll explore why and how grace made a way for you to receive a new and better relationship with God—one based on better promises than the Old Testament saints dreamed possible. You'll discover one grace-gift called righteousness that changes everything about the way we live, love, and worship. We'll unwrap a gift called Sabbath rest and learn why we all need it so very desperately. Most important of all, you're about to discover the greatest (and perhaps most neglected) of all grace's gifts. The gift of adoption. The one that makes us not servants in God's fields but rather sons and daughters at His banqueting table. These and many other gifts are waiting to be unveiled.

At times, you may be tempted to argue with the words on the page. You may want to shout, "That can't possibly be right! That sounds too good to be true!" If so, then it's a good sign you're at least getting close to the truth about your heavenly Father. The human intellect staggers at the immensity of His love and kindness. Our finite imaginations can't begin to comprehend just how good and generous He is. But even as your mind reels, your born-again spirit will leap up within you in thrilled recognition of divine truth. Your spirit knows the truth when it hears it.

For too long we've been like that poor, sweet woman Debbie and I tried to bless that day. We've not known how to receive a gift given in love. We've preferred to try to *earn*. To *merit*. To strive, in some pitifully inadequate way. To *deserve*. We've wanted to add works to grace. But as you're about to discover, the only way to honor God's generosity is to receive it with open arms and a heart filled with gratitude. To do otherwise is to rob Him of joy. Giving to those He loves is what delights your heavenly Father. As Jesus said in Luke 12:32: "Do not fear, little flock, for it is your Father's good pleasure to give you the kingdom."

What you now hold in your hands is a 256-page testament to the extraordinary generosity of our God and the unfathomable depths of His love. Those pages contain truths, insights, and life-giving revelations presented in a very deliberate, three-part sequence. Yes, I am about to take you on a voyage with a specific itinerary in mind.

Our ultimate destination is a place of rest and hope and peace and fruitfulness. But we first must explore the biblical concept of grace itself. The word *grace* is so commonly thrown around in Christian circles that it seemingly can mean anything and everything. So the first part of this book brings you a look at the many facets of the blindingly brilliant gem that is true, authentic, biblical grace.

Only then are you prepared to understand what grace, and only grace, made possible. I'm referring to a set of glorious, unconditional blessings springing from infinite unconditional love. Or to use the language of the author of the book of Hebrews, "a better covenant based on better promises" (see Chapter 8, v. 6). This eye-opening stop makes up the second part of this three-part book.

Yet all of that is only a prelude to the main attraction on this trip. Grace and a grace-saturated new covenant were never God's final intention. They were merely a means to achieving His real goal—one we'll explore in the third part of this work. There we'll discover that God did not send Jesus to restore us to good behavior. Instead, He gave His best and most precious to restore us to Himself. The goal of grace is restoring us back to intimate connection as delighted-in sons and daughters of a good Father.

For God, the treasure at the end of his story of grace is *you*. It seems we have much to learn about how to respond to Him and receive from Him. Let's get started, shall we?

PART 1

AMAZING, PERIOD.

CHAPTER 1

WHAT'S SO AMAZING?

Wait...What?...Are these guys really arguing about grace? Really? Grace!?

That was my bewildered, unspoken question at one point during my first week of Bible college. I was nineteen and delighted to be at *any* college, much less one with "Bible" in its name. Why? Well, not only was I new to sensing a call to ministry, I was new to being saved!

It hadn't been all that long before that I'd knelt down in a humble little roadside motel room and completely given my life to Jesus. I was already married at that point and for reasons known only to her and an omniscient God, Debbie—the sweetest, godliest girl East Texas had ever produced—had agreed to marry me even though I was a reprobate. Sure, I had been raised in a Christian home by two of the finest human beings on the planet. And had been dragged to church until I was too big to drag. But I was still utterly lost until that day of surrender at Jake's Motel.

Anyone who knew me in high school could not be blamed for predicting that I was destined for prison after graduation. (Fortunately, our yearbook didn't have a category for "Most Likely to Serve Hard Time or End Up Dead Behind a Convenience Store.") Yet there I was in Bible college clearly sensing a call to ministry. I was excited and zealous and idealistic in the way only brand-new believers can be. I'd arrived on the campus overjoyed to be cleansed, forgiven, and called, and half expecting everyone else there to be holding hands and singing Maranatha worship songs between classes. *After all*, I reasoned, *surely everyone here is more spiritually mature and therefore more spiritual than I am.*

Which explains my shock when, upon entering one of the common areas, I stumbled into the middle of a heated argument among a huddle of upperclassmen—theology majors, I soon discovered. The debate was over the nature of God's grace. One was holding forth for Tertullian's view of grace. Another advocated for the Augustinian view. While still another championed John Calvin's Efficacious Grace concept. Several more views were also represented in the increasingly angry debate. One red-faced guy was hissing at another about being a "Pelagian!" I didn't know what that was, but from the way he said it through gritted teeth, I was pretty sure it wasn't a good thing to be.

It's difficult to communicate how dumbfounded I was by this incident. All I knew about grace was that it was wonderful beyond my feeble human ability to describe. One moment I had been an angry, self-destructive, profane young man. Then an encounter with grace changed everything. I'd heard the song "Amazing Grace" sung countless times growing up. But now I actually understood what everyone else had been singing about through tear-filled eyes all those years. I really

> All I knew about grace was that it was wonderful beyond my feeble human ability to describe.

had been a wretch, and He saved me. Me! I really had been lost but now was found. I really had been blind but now could see!

I stood there speechless. But what I wanted to do was stand up on a chair and say, "Guys! If you only knew where I was... *who* I was... just a year or two ago... if you understood that I shouldn't even be alive and standing here today, much less in a Bible college studying for the ministry... you wouldn't be arguing about minor differences in your definitions of grace. You'd be as much in awe of God's goodness as I am. Grace is the kindness and mercy and generosity of God on glorious display!" Looking back, I wish I had done that.

Grace is a truth so simple yet so profound. The great nineteenth-century preacher Charles Spurgeon described that contrast this way:

> Come, Believer, and contemplate this sublime Truth of God, thus proclaimed to you in simple monosyllables—"He... laid... down... His... life... for... us." There is not one long word in the sentence—it is all as simple as it can be—and it is simple because it is sublime.[1]

He's right. Familiarity with the old hymn has numbed our hearts to the power of the phrase, but it is true nonetheless. Grace is truly *amazing*. Indeed, it's overwhelming when you ponder it. And pondering it is what we will do throughout the pages of this book. That's my mission here. To overwhelm you with revelation about the grace of God. But not just for the sake of stirring your emotions.

A deeper, fuller understanding of grace will change you. For one thing, it will fill you with thankfulness. That's important because a heart of gratitude is a powerful key to living a great life in God. But grasping grace will do even more in you. It will move you into a place of rest and peace in your relationship with God. It will increase your confidence before Him, thereby elevating your closeness and intimacy with Him. And believe me when I tell you, the more intimately acquainted you become with your heavenly Father, the better everything in your life will go. You'll be more fruitful, more joyful, more sensitive to the promptings of the Holy Spirit, and much, much more, as you'll discover in the chapters ahead.

> A deeper, fuller understanding of grace will change you.

It wasn't that long ago that I sensed a prompting from the Holy Spirit to write this book. I recall saying to the Lord at that time, "Okay, Lord, why a book on grace? And why now?"

I know my Father's voice. And His reply to me was clear and full of passion:

Look around, Robert. Just look around you. How many people—believers included—don't know the reality of My grace? How many of My blood-bought children needlessly trudge through their days with weights of shame and condemnation hanging around their necks? How many of My people never realize their full potential in Me because of a fear of failure? How many of My beloved people are exhausted from trying to perform for Me or earn My love? How many live lives of endless discouragement and shame because they fail over and over to live up to an impossible standard? How many are experiencing something far, far below the "abundant life" I sent and sacrificed My only begotten Son to purchase for them? *That's* why I need you to write a book about My amazing grace, son!

So here I am, bringing you good news—the best news in the world, actually. It's an assignment I relish. I love talking about the abundant, lavish, extravagant grace of God. You see, you cannot understand God without grasping grace. You cannot understand the gospel without grasping grace. You cannot live the fruitful, impactful, peaceful, joy-filled life that Jesus made possible without grasping, embracing, and placing your trust in the truth about grace. You just can't. It truly is amazing. So my goal here is to help you realize how truly amazing grace really is. I want you to be as overwhelmed by it as I am.

In the process, we'll address some of the most common misunderstandings about grace. So many of God's sons and daughters have absorbed well-intentioned but wrong teaching about grace. Please note what Paul said in Colossians 2:6, "So then, just as you received Christ Jesus as Lord, continue to live your lives in him" (NIV). In other words, we continue in God the very same way we started in Him.

The unadulterated truth is that we are *saved* by grace and grace alone. And we must *live* this Christian life the same way. By grace and grace alone.

Not grace *and*…

Not grace *with*…

Not grace *plus*…

Not grace *but*…

The key to experiencing the extraordinary life Jesus came and died to make possible for you is this: Grace…Period.

CHAPTER 2

GIFT, WAGE, OR REWARD?

Brace yourself. I am about to drop a startling bit of useful information on you. This is a truth vast numbers of people around the world seem to have forgotten. Ready?

It's possible to remain friends with someone who disagrees with you about something important to you.

Hopefully someone revived you with smelling salts after reading that previous sentence. Yes, it's true. Sadly, the age of social media and the extreme polarization it has fostered have made that a forgotten truth. It is tough to overstate how much the ability to "unfriend" someone with the click of a finger has transformed our relationships and culture. As many have observed, a lot of us now live in self-made information bubbles. We choose who we want to hear from on social media and choose news and information sources that serve only to validate what we already think. These are tightly managed echo chambers in which we never have to experience the discomfort of hearing something we don't like.

I mention this because I have a great friend; and one time I thought we had a disagreement, but as we talked, I found out we

9

actually didn't. But we were committed to staying friends no matter what. He shared an illustration that I thought he meant that we had to work to get to heaven. So as friends do, we got together to talk about it. I had heard that he had shared an illustration about grace, and I had totally misunderstood it. And the problem was, "I had heard that he shared an illustration," but I had not actually heard him share it, so when we got together, things got cleared up pretty quickly!

I had heard that he had shared an illustration that we were in a boat, and we were given a set of oars, and those oars were grace, and if we ever stopped rowing, we would go to hell! As we shared, we found out our understanding and teachings about grace were identical! We both believe that there is nothing we can do to earn our salvation and that work would not somehow keep us saved, but that we are saved by grace and grace alone (or in other words, Grace. Period.)

We laughed and had a great lunch and remain best friends to this day! He is a great man of God and a great Bible Teacher in the Body of Christ. He completely understood my concern because there are many believers raised in a law-based religious system who believe grace is God's ability to keep the law and if we ever stop working, we are in deep trouble. If that were the case, then I messed up the first day after I was saved, and many days since!

Years ago, a sermon I heard contained another illustration that was supposed to explain the role of grace in salvation and living the Christian life. I was told that our journey through life is like a large lake, with heaven lying on the opposite shore. Those who wish to be Christians are handed two oars. (I think that's why I jumped to the conclusion when I thought my friend was going down the same road.)

In this illustration, one oar was grace and the other oar was good works and/or good behavior. I was told that the only way to get across the lake (to heaven) was to use *both* oars. The speaker obviously anticipated an objection based on Ephesians 2:8, some of the most familiar and wonderful words in all the New Testament: "For by grace you have been saved through faith, and that not of yourselves."

So this preacher said, "Of course grace is necessary. You can't get to heaven on works alone. If you try to row across the lake with the oar of works only, you'll just go around in circles! But the same is true if you only use the oar of grace." The point was that you have to add an adequate amount of good works, good behavior, and human effort to God's grace in order to make it all the way across.

The terrifying implication of that metaphor, if accurate, is that it's possible to spend your whole life rowing as hard as you can, but if you quit doing all the stuff—even if you're only ten yards from shore— you're disqualified. And make no mistake, the terror is precisely the point of that illustration. Many mistakenly believe that fear is a necessary motivator to keep themselves and other believers toeing the line. Fear of hell, fear of rejection (by God), fear of punishment, fear of not being good enough in your behavior and fervent enough in your faith to receive anything good from God. It's all a prescription for a life of torment. (By the way, my friend has the best teaching on the fear of God that I've ever heard.) Yet didn't Jesus say He came that we might have abundant life? (See John 10:10.)

> Many mistakenly believe that fear is a necessary motivator to keep themselves and other believers toeing the line.

Living in this kind of fear is a form of bondage. And yet Paul clearly tells you, me, and all believers this:

> For you did not *receive the spirit of bondage again to fear*, but you received the Spirit of adoption by whom we cry out, "Abba, Father." The Spirit Himself bears witness with our spirit that we are children of God. (Romans 8:15–16)

Our examination of grace will destroy this false metaphor about what grace is and how it works. And that examination should begin with the word itself.

The Greek word translated "grace" in our English New Testaments is usually *charis*. It has a couple of cousins—*charisma* and *charismata*, which also make numerous appearances in our Bibles. We'll visit all of these before we're finished. But we'll begin with the one that appears more than 140 times in the New Testament: *charis*.

Strong's Concordance—pretty much the gold standard for Greek in the realm of biblical reference materials—tells us this about *charis*:

Definition: grace, kindness

Usage: (a) grace, as a gift or blessing brought to man by Jesus Christ, (b) favor, (c) gratitude, thanks, (d) a favor, kindness[2]

Notice the word *gift* in the first description under "Usage." It's there for good reason. Other ancient Greek writers might have used the word *charis* in a variety of ways, but the people who penned the books of your New Testament—all writing under the inspiration and direction of the Holy Spirit—used the word in a similar way.

And that use always carries the implication of a gift. A gift of something good and lovely and of value. The kind of gift a loving Father would bestow on a beloved child.

The entry for *charis* in the *Dictionary of Biblical Languages: Greek* includes "kindness, gift, thanks, good will, and favor toward someone" in its definition.[3] Again we see the word *gift*.

The related word *charisma* makes the connection to the concept of gift plain. It literally means "grace-gift" and occurs seventeen times in the New Testament.

Once you begin to grasp that the concept of gift sits at the heart of the biblical word *grace*, everything comes into focus. You see you can only do two things with a gift. You can either receive it or reject it. You can earn wages. You can merit rewards. You can purchase anything you desire as long as you have enough of the correct currency.

> Once you begin to grasp that the concept of gift sits at the heart of the biblical word *grace*, everything comes into focus.

But a gift can only be accepted.

And so it is with grace—and every good thing the Bible says God bestows through grace. At the top of this glorious list is salvation itself. Look with fresh eyes at Ephesians 2:8–9 again, this time from The Passion Translation:

> For by grace you have been saved by faith. Nothing you did could ever earn this salvation, for it was the love gift from God that brought us to Christ! So no one will ever be able to boast, for salvation is never a reward for good works or human striving.

Now that we know what grace is, let me share my preferred definition. Ready?

Grace is the unmerited, undeserved, unearned kindness and favor of God.

There is a ton of life-changing truth in that eleven-word sentence. So let's unpack it by examining each of the three key adjectives. We'll begin with *unmerited*.

CHAPTER 3

AMAZINGLY UNMERITED

The Bible word is *boasting*. But in my home state of Texas, we call it *bragging*.

It's a word that reminds me of a famous quote by Major League Baseball pitcher Dizzy Dean. Dean's heyday was the late 1930s. He was born in 1910 in a tiny town in the hills of Arkansas called Lucas, and never finished fourth grade. But Jay "Dizzy" Dean grew up to become one of the greatest major-league pitchers of that era. He was also an expert in the verbal art form modern athletes call trash talking. He loved to make audacious predictions about what he was going to do in an upcoming game. And more often than not, he delivered on his predictions. Which brings me to the iconic quote—one often repeated in the world of sports to this day—that will forever be associated with Dizzy. After being accused by a reporter of bragging, Dean famously replied:

"Hey, it ain't braggin' if you can really do it."

Now, far be it from me to question the logic or semantics of a Hall of Fame pitcher, but Dizzy's statement is simply untrue. In fact, it's the opposite of true. In reality, it's bragging if, and only if, you *can* actually do whatever it is you claim you can do. Otherwise, it's just bluffing. Or the less polite term: lying through your teeth.

Think about it. Suppose I had memorized the book of Acts and could recite all 24,229 words of it from memory. (I can't, but go with me here for the purpose of illustration.) Also suppose that I tended to tell everyone I encountered that I could do so. Imagine that I looked for creative ways to work it into the conversation with acquaintances, and would approach random strangers in order to share the exciting news of my ability. "Hi, I'm Robert Morris. I've memorized the entire book of Acts!"

Sorry, Dizzy, but that *would* be bragging. Or to use the biblical term, boasting.

We tend to think of boasting as an indicator of pride. And it can be. But more often than not, it's actually outward evidence of inward insecurity. The fact is, pride and insecurity are really just two sides of the same coin. People who are secure in their identities rarely brag. They don't feel the need to. It's the guy who won't stop talking about his skills and accomplishments who is likely the most insecure person in the room. The chest-beating and self-aggrandizement reveal a desperate need to be viewed by others as significant.

So why this journey from Dizzy Dean to Psychology 101? Because we're exploring the definition of *grace* I offered at the end of the previous chapter:

Grace is the unmerited, undeserved, unearned kindness and favor of God.

That exploration must begin with the first of those three key words. We need an understanding that grace is unmerited.

If you were in Boy Scouts or Girl Scouts when you were younger, you recall the never-ending quest for merit badges. And no doubt you also recall the feeling of pride and accomplishment that came from qualifying for that Camping, Signaling, Dog Care, or Astronomy merit badge. Today those vintage merit badges with the colorful embroidered symbols are highly collectible. And of course, some clever entrepreneurs have built businesses out of selling nostalgic adults fake, comical, authentic-looking merit badges in specialties such as Snoring, Computer Viruses, Text Messaging, Whining, Boat Sinking, and Duct Tape.

The whole merit-badge system was built upon every human being's innate desire to achieve and our hunger to be recognized for having done so. It's not a bad thing to want to master new skills and be recognized for all the hard work and accomplishment. As we'll see a little later on in this journey, even with spiritual things, there is a place for going after rewards. But this can never be the case with salvation, or with any other grace-gift God wants to bestow upon us in His kindness and generosity. Remember, if it's truly a gift, there are only two things you can do with it: receive it or reject it.

Which brings us again to Ephesians 2:8–9. Here it is again broken down by its phrases, for clarity:

- For by grace you have been saved
- through faith,
- and that not of yourselves;
- it is the gift of God,
- not of works,
- lest anyone should boast.

Remember, if you can do it yourself, or can contribute to it in any way, you're boasting (bragging) when you talk about it. But here the Word of God plainly tells us that no one can rightly boast about being saved. Why? Because salvation is a grace-gift.

In other words...there's no rowing involved! If you row—whether it's with one oar or two—in order to contribute to your salvation, you've merited it in some way, and you therefore have some room to boast.

Please understand me here. There will be no boasting in heaven.

Sure, there is plenty of boasting on earth right now. Boasting over accomplishments small and great, noble and stupid. But there will be none in heaven. Of the billions of souls you'll encounter there, not one will be heard saying, "I'm so glad I kept rowing. Yay, me! Sure, I got weary at times but I didn't quit! I kept adding my effort and striving to God's grace. And that's why I'm here. I had some friends who didn't keep rowing and you'll notice they're not here. But I'm here because I rowed hard and rowed well."

No, nothing like that will enter your mind there. Here's what you and every other blood-washed adopted son and daughter of God will do upon entering the glories of eternity. You'll point to the nail marks in Jesus' hands. You'll point to the horrific scars on His back. And you'll say, "You see those. That's why I'm here! *He's* why I'm here. It was all Him!"

> There will be no salvation merit badge in heaven. Why? Because salvation is by grace and is therefore *unmerited.*

There will be no salvation merit badge in heaven. Why? Because salvation is by grace and is therefore *unmerited.*

Believers like me who were saved as adults understand something that people like my wife who were born again as children might not. When you've lived in sinfulness and depravity for years and then encounter the extravagant mercy of God—a mercy made available only through the enormous sacrifice of His sinless Son—you *know* you don't merit it. At first. But fast-forward twenty years. After the love of God has transformed your desires and habits…after you've done some good things…after you've made church attendance a part of your weekly routine…it's a perilously easy thing to start thinking that, somehow, you've begun to merit some blessing, some favor, and maybe even heaven. Pride is always and ever ready to ooze in through the unhealed cracks and crevices of our hearts.

No, the truth is that even our righteousness is as filthy rags (see Isaiah 64:6). The best thing about you is not even close to the worst thing about God. Take the best day you've ever had in terms of good works and good behavior and it all is still pitifully inadequate. Imagine that the pristine righteousness and holiness necessary to stand in God's presence is the summit of Mount Everest. Your worst day is ground level and your best day ever is only half an inch up the mountain.

That's the severe beauty of grace. There's no place for pride or boasting anywhere in the equation. What comes from God by grace is always and only…unmerited.

When I think about this aspect of grace, I'm reminded of something my grown son, Josh, reminded me of not too long ago. We were talking about the amazing nature of God's grace and he said, "Dad, I think I've had an easier time grasping grace than a lot of other believers I know because you modeled

> That's the severe beauty of grace. There's no place for pride or boasting anywhere in the equation.

it for us when we were kids." He went on to remind me of an incident when he was in junior high.

The day came when everyone received their yearbooks. He and a
couple of friends thought it would be hilarious to spend their lunch
break drawing mustaches, beards, or horns on the photos of all their
teachers, along with other juvenile defacements of many of the pic-
tures. When he got home at the end of the day, I saw him carrying it
and said, "Hey, you got your yearbook! Let me see it!" Suddenly all
the color drained out of his face. He clutched it tighter and started
stammering while inching toward his bedroom. After some insis-
tence, he showed it to me and, of course, I saw all the supplemental
artwork. In recalling the memory, he said I got a sad look on my
face and said, "Son, do you realize what you've done? Not only is
this disrespectful to the teachers who spent a whole year trying to
help you, this yearbook is something you're going to want to look
back on years from now. But you ruined it."

Josh always had a tender heart. When the reality of that hit, he
burst into tears. He remembers me picking his chin up and saying, "Son, look at me. Tomorrow, I'm going to buy you a new one."
He looked shocked and sputtered out, "Why...why would you do
that?"

"Because that's what fathers do, son."

Marking up a brand-new yearbook is the kind of stupid act I
specialized in when I was that age. And my father modeled grace,
too. You're certainly familiar with the Scripture that says, "Love will
cover a multitude of sins" (1 Peter 4:8). Well, here's a verse from the
Book of Robert: "Grace will cover a multitude of stupid mistakes."
Have you ever done anything stupid? I suspect so. Then be grateful
for grace.

Now, many people confuse grace with mercy. This will help

you see and understand the difference. Not punishing Josh for that stunt was mercy. But buying him a new yearbook? Well, that was grace. Why? Because it was a gift that was utterly unmerited. A gift extended with love from a father's heart.

Grace is, indeed, unmerited. But that's not all it is.

CHAPTER 4

AMAZINGLY UNDESERVED

We're defining *grace*, and so far we have explored only one of three facets of this brilliant diamond. We know now that grace is unmerited. We've also seen that the Greek word translated "grace" in our English Bibles is *charis*. It's time to take a deeper dive into the meaning of that Greek term.

Let's start with pronunciation! Most Americans pronounce the word like it begins with a hard *k* sound and with the accent on the first syllable. As in *KAIR-iss*. And that's okay. That'll work. But it does remind me of a funny incident with a friend of mine. His last name was Maddox and he was excitedly telling me he had a baby daughter on the way. Of course, I asked if he and his wife had chosen a name yet. He said "Yes! We're going to name her Charis!" He then watched a smile begin to spread across my face. "What?" he asked. "Why are you smiling?"

"Have you said her full name out loud?" I asked.

So he proceeded to say it. "Charis Maddox . . . Charis Maddox . . . Charis Maddox . . ." On the third or fourth saying, the light came on. He realized that to the ear, it sounded identical to *charismatics*.

Not that there's anything wrong with charismatics. I'm one myself! But if you're going to give that name to your baby girl, you should probably do so with your eyes open.

Technically, that Greek word is pronounced *kha-REECE*. And if you are really going to say it correctly, you need to say the *kh* sound like you have one of those little fish bones stuck in your throat. It's very similar to the beginning of the proper pronunciation of *Hannukah* or *Channukah*. However, to simplify things, you can pronounce *charis* in your head any way you want for the remainder of this book. The more important thing is to understand what Paul and the other inspired biblical writers *meant* when they used that word, and what their original readers understood when they saw it. Yes, most people in the first-century world of the Bible spoke Greek. This had been the case for nearly four hundred years—ever since Alexander the Great conquered a huge chunk of the known world and established the Greek Empire. So when the typical reader of Ephesians 2:8 saw, "For by [*charis*] you have been saved, through faith…" that word carried a very specific bundle of meanings, references, and images. In other words, *charis* was a well-known cultural term long before it first appeared in a book of the Bible.

For historical light on the meaning of this extraordinary and important word, we need to travel back in time for a bit.

It is the year A.D. 15 and Tiberius has recently been named emperor of the vast Roman Empire following the death of Caesar Augustus. In the eastern end of the empire, in what will one day be the nation of Turkey, lies the province of Galatia. There, a farmer named Silvanus is in desperate trouble. For the third year in a row, an entire crop of olives from his family plot of olive trees has catastrophically failed. Some strange invading moth, seemingly crafted in the pit of hell, has invaded his orchards.

After the first two failed harvests, Silvanus was able to keep his large family afloat through his savings. Now, following a third consecutive disaster, his savings are exhausted. If he doesn't acquire some capital quickly, he will be forced to sell—at a fraction of its real value—the land and groves that have been in his family for a dozen generations. His only hope is a centuries-old system the Romans adopted from their predecessors, the Greeks—the patronage system. Economically, both cultures—Greek and Roman—were characterized by a thin layer of ultra-wealthy elites and almost everyone else subsisting as the working poor. In other words, what we call the middle class was almost nonexistent. So in these cultures, a practice developed in which a poor person, known in Latin as the *cliens* (this is where we get our word *client*), approached a wealthy person, who in this system was called the *patronus* (patron). A potential client would approach a potential patron with a specific need. That need might be for help in the legal system, help in arranging a good marriage for a son or daughter, or often, as in the case of our olive farmer, Silvanus, a desperate need for money. Whatever the request was, there was a word in the patronage system for the act of meeting that need: *charis*!

When a person in desperate need of help found a patron willing to show them favor and generosity, that help was *charis*, or, put another way, unmerited, undeserved favor that resulted in a gift that met the need.

In ancient Rome, being in the position to be a patron was a major source of social prestige. If you were a patron who had lots of "clients," it was a sign that you were simultaneously very rich and very generous. And as in elite society circles in every place and era, everyone wanted others to perceive them as fabulously rich and wildly generous. In our day, it would be like being the kind of person who enjoys being invited to the black-tie, $1,000-per-plate fundraising gala to fund a new wing of the local art museum.

Here is the problem for our new friend Silvanus. He doesn't know any potential patrons. Rural olive grove farmers with dirty fingernails just don't rub shoulders with the ultra-elite of the big city. But all is not lost! This is where the role of another player in the Roman patron-client system emerges. Silvanus needed a *sectorem*. That's a Latin word that roughly translates in English to "broker." Today a broker is an intermediary, or middleman, in a transaction or deal. In Silvanus's day, a *sectorem* was a person who was high enough in society to know and have relationships with rich potential patrons, but who also moved freely among the lower class of society. Thus, this person, if willing to help, could connect you to a patron and help make your case for you.

Fortunately, Silvanus knows someone who knows someone who knows a *sectorem* or broker. An introduction is arranged. The broker is moved with compassion at Silvanus's pitiful plight. Miracle of miracles, the broker finds a patron willing to extend *charis* to the desperate farmer. The gift is delivered. Silvanus and his family maintain possession of the land, and in the years that follow, the harvests return to normal.

Now, you may be wondering what kinds of strings were attached to this undeserved *charis* gift? It may surprise you to learn that in the patronage system there is no formal obligation to repay. What *is* expected is that the recipient of *charis* will be profoundly grateful.

And as a result, they will love and be loyal to the patron. Of course, for the vast majority of people, gratitude is the natural response to being given a life-changing gift that was free and undeserved. It was also understood by all parties that the extension of this *charis* created an ongoing connection between two (or three if a broker was involved) parties. In other words, the process created a *relationship*. The giver and receiver were now connected relationally for life. Clearly, *charis* was (and is) a big deal! In a sense, the patron became a father to the client. The client became a son to the patron. Is it any mystery why Paul and the other New Testament writers chose *charis* to describe what God had done through His son, Jesus Christ?

Now, dear reader, with an understanding of the ancient patron-broker-client custom, you have a much better sense of what the first-century readers of the New Testament immediately thought of when they encountered the word *charis* in passages such as Ephesians 2:8–9. Let me paraphrase that familiar verse in a way that incorporates our new understanding:

For by a *charis* from a patron-God, who is unfathomably rich and unspeakably kind, you have been rescued from eternal spiritual bankruptcy, through faith, and even that faith was not your own, it too was a gift. Which is why there is no room for bragging or boasting about your newfound relationship as a friend of the patron.

I suspect you also are way ahead of me about who the broker is in the biblical version of *charis*. Clearly, Jesus played the role of the *sectorem* in extending the gift of redeeming grace to you and me. He left the side of the patron in heaven and came to walk among us in the dirt and grime of earth. We didn't know God, the patron.

But He did. (By the way, the Latin word for "father" is *pater.*) And through His sacrificial death and resurrection, He made a way for us to connect to the Father and receive the most extravagant free gift ever offered. No wonder Paul used the term *charis*! Yes, the ancient patronage system paints a beautiful picture of what God did for us, but it's not a perfect picture. You see, everything God does is better and sweeter than anything man can come up with.

Here is where the secular patron-broker-client model for understanding *charis* breaks down. In ancient Greece and Rome, patrons did not come looking for poor clients to bless and help. No, the client had to go looking for the patron. Yet our magnificent patron, our heavenly Father, came looking for us! Just as He came looking for Adam and Eve in the Garden of Eden. Think about it. When Adam and Eve betrayed their Maker and followed the lead of His mortal enemy, the serpent, they didn't go looking for God. On the contrary, they hid from Him. Yet God came looking for them!

The same was true for you, me, and all of Adam and Eve's offspring. God sent His only Son as the broker so we could be reconnected to Him in relationship. "Jesus sought me when a stranger..." the old hymn "Come, Thou Fount of Every Blessing" rightly proclaims. As Jesus Himself proclaimed in Luke 19:10: "For the Son of Man has come to seek and to save that which was lost."

No wealthy patron or broker in ancient Rome ever went looking for the most destitute, most bankrupt, most irresponsible, most hopeless

> No wealthy patron or broker in ancient Rome ever went looking for the most destitute, most bankrupt, most irresponsible, most hopeless beggars to bless and flood with undeserved kindness.

beggars to bless and flood with undeserved kindness. Yet that is precisely what the Father and Son did for you and me. Out of unfathomable love the patron sent the broker to find us and rescue us:

For God did not send His Son into the world to condemn the world, but that the world through Him might be saved. (John 3:17)

In another passage Jesus compared each of us to a lost sheep, a lost coin, and a lost son—all searched for and rejoiced over when found—in order to describe His mission and purpose. By the way, we'll be mining those parables for spiritual gold later on in this book. Yes, *charis* is the right word, but in God's hands this earthly system became one in which the giver sought out those of us who desperately need His generosity.

But God, being rich in mercy, because of the great love with which he loved us, even when we were dead in our trespasses, made us alive together with Christ—by grace [*charis*] you have been saved [rescued]. (Ephesians 2:4–5 ESV, additions mine)

Now you understand why the second aspect of *charis* (grace) is that it is undeserved. We don't deserve it any more than Silvanus deserved to be helped by his patron. Silvanus was empty-handed, with nothing to offer his patron except a lifetime of gratitude. As Paul reminds us:

For when we were still without strength, in due time Christ died for the ungodly. For scarcely for a righteous man will one die; yet perhaps for a good man someone would even dare to die. But God demonstrates His own love toward us, in that while we were still sinners, Christ died for us. (Romans 5:6–8)

Yes, God's grace is wholly unmerited and completely undeserved. But that's not all it is. We still have another facet of this jewel to examine. And it's a wonderful one!

CHAPTER 5

AMAZINGLY UNEARNED

It's your birthday and you're surrounded by friends. It's time to open presents. You grab a large package, and the friend who brought it beams. You open it up and are delighted by what you find inside. You look at your friend and are about to say thank you when he or she says, "That'll be $89.95! No, wait... actually you owe me $97.37 with tax."

That's ridiculous, right? That's not the way gifts work. Well, unless you're a parent. I can remember a few Father's Days in which my kids were allowed to pick out my gifts. In those cases I tended to have two questions. One: "What is it?" And two: "How much did I pay for this?" I'm joking of course. My point is: Gifts are free. If you have to pay for it, it is not a gift in any meaningful sense of the word.

This brings us to the third aspect of authentic, biblical grace. It is unearned. Wages are earned but grace, by its very nature, never is. Our sins and our sinfulness is, in a sense, a debt to divine justice. Grace is the payment, by God, of that massive debt we had no power to ever pay.

The truth is that every one of us was born with an unpaid debt to God's eternal, immutable justice. A debt we inherited from our forefather Adam. An obligation we then added to with our own sinfulness and rebellion. Then a second "Adam" came along, walked into the cashier's office of the courts of heaven, and paid every last cent of it off. We contributed nothing to that debt cancellation. It was completely and utterly unearned.

Paul had this reality in mind when he wrote:

> And you, who were dead in your trespasses and the uncircumcision of your flesh, God made alive together with him, having forgiven us all our trespasses, by *canceling the record of debt that stood against us* with its legal demands. This he set aside, nailing it to the cross. (Colossians 2:13–14 ESV, emphasis added)

When I ponder this extraordinary truth, I can't help but think of a powerful story I heard told by the late, great preacher Dr. E. V. Hill—longtime pastor of the iconic Mount Zion Missionary Baptist Church in Los Angeles—when I was a young man. The gravel-voiced African American preacher was speaking at a conference I was attending, and his testimony made a powerful impression on a skinny young country boy sensing a call to preach.

Born in 1933, in the depths of the Great Depression, Dr. Hill grew up on the other side of the tracks in a tiny Texas town about seventy-five miles west of Houston. From the platform of that conference he shared how, when he was a child, he told his mother, "I want to be a pastor when I grow up." His mother's immediate, affirming response was, "Well, then you'll need to go to college. Plan on doing that." He accepted her words, and from that point forward assumed that after high school, he'd head off to college just as seamlessly as one would move from middle school to high school. But only as he approached high school graduation did the economic realities of going to college come into focus for him.

Once he got some insight into the costs of college and became aware of his family's poverty, his assumptions about college began to crumble. Not wanting his mother to feel a financial burden she couldn't possibly carry, he recalled one conversation that went this way:

"Mom, I'm still planning to be a pastor, but I may not go to college."

"Son, you're going to college."

"Mom, I've looked into the costs. We can't even afford the books, much less the tuition and housing."

She looked him right in the eye and said, "Son, God will provide."

Indeed, every time he brought that matter up to his mother, her response was the same. "Son, God will provide."

Eventually, the day came to register at Prairieview A&M near Houston. With great trepidation and uncertainty, he got on a bus and headed to the campus. Upon arrival, he went to the administration building and got in line at the registrar's office. He watched with a rising sense of panic as each student in front of him pulled out money to pay for their first semester of schooling. He had little more than loose change in his pocket. Yet beneath the noise of his emotional turmoil, he could faintly hear his mother's voice saying, "God will provide."

Soon, he found himself at the front of the line. Dry-mouthed, perspiring, and speechless, Dr. Hill seriously considered running for the door. In fact, he was about to do so when the man behind the counter looked up and said, "Name?"

"Edward Victor Hill," he managed to whisper.

The man seemed to recognize the name, fumbled around on his desk for a minute, and then produced an envelope. He handed it to Hill, who opened it and found a letter granting him a full and complete four-year scholarship. Along with the letter, the envelope contained a handwritten note:

God will provide!

Then the registrar took the invoice for Dr. Hill's first semester of books, tuition, room, and meals and stamped it PAID IN FULL.

I can't look at those three words on the page without thinking about one of Jesus' final statements from the cross. His final words were, "Father, into Your hands I commit my spirit" (Luke 22:46). But right before that He'd shouted something that rang through the canyons around Jerusalem and echoed off her ancient walls. He'd shouted a single Greek word:

Tetelestai!

Our English translations of the Scriptures tend to render the word *tetelestai* as, "It is finished." And that's not wrong, but it is inadequate. In the ancient Greek-speaking world, *tetelestai* was also written on business documents or transaction receipts to indicate that a bill or debt had been fully satisfied.

Doesn't that put our Savior's shout from the cross in a new light? In the moment before giving up His spirit in death, after suffering unimaginable pain and shame and abandonment, Jesus did more than just say, "This process is complete." No, he was stamping your debt and my debt with a stamp, dipped in blood-red ink, PAID IN FULL.

In this light we can begin to comprehend how insulting it is when we try to earn, or merit, or pay. Please recall the dear woman I mentioned in the "Start Here" introduction to this book. The one

> When God, by grace, gives us salvation, favor, help, deliverance, rescue, or any other good and perfect gift, it insults His grace to treat it as if it is a wage to be earned rather than a free gift to be received.

who, when given an extravagant gift, quickly turned to trying to find a way to pay us back. When God, by grace, gives us salvation, favor, help, deliverance, rescue, or any other good and perfect gift, it insults His grace to treat it as if it is a wage to be earned rather than a free gift to be received. *Free* is the key word in that previous sentence. If it is earned, then it is not free. If it is free, then it is not earned.

Several years ago, I saw a report about a remarkable father and son who painted the most vivid picture I've ever encountered concerning how God's gift works in our lives.

The report was a profile of Dick and Rick Hoyt. Rick was born with the umbilical cord around his neck, which resulted in his brain being deprived of oxygen for a time during labor and delivery. This left Rick severely physically disabled—unable to walk or talk. As he grew, the Hoyts discovered that Rick could communicate with them by moving his eyes. He ultimately learned to read and write using a special computer tablet and keyboard. Rick Hoyt was one of the first people on the planet to be fitted with and use such a device.

When Rick was fifteen, he learned that a school classmate had been paralyzed in an accident. He then learned that the school was organizing a 5k run to raise money for the classmate's medical costs. Using his tablet and keyboard, Rick indicated to his father that he wanted to participate in that race. So Dick Hoyt, who was not a runner, began training to prepare to push his wheelchair-bound son in the little 5k race. Afterward, Rick was jubilant. He said, "Dad, that was the first time in my whole life that I did not feel handicapped."

This inspired Dick to offer his son that experience again. And then again. Additional 5ks and then 10ks and ultimately marathons followed. In each one, Dick pushed Rick the entire distance. As if marathons weren't enough, the two eventually graduated to triathlons! A triathlon, if you don't know, is a 2.4-mile swim followed by a full 26.2-mile marathon followed by a 112-mile bicycle ride. In the swimming portion, Dick swam while towing Rick on a raft. For the bicycling portion, Dick pedaled a custom-built bike with a seat on the front for Rick.

Dick died at the age of eighty in 2021, but before his body gave out, he and Rick had run seventy-two marathons and 255 triathlons.

That, my friend, is a picture of grace. A loving, compassionate Father carrying us into places we could never go ourselves. Do you see it? You and I are in the chair. Any good or anything of value we've done is wholly because the Father's been pushing, towing, and carrying us the whole way. We have nothing to contribute except our willingness to receive. We're standing at the registrar window with empty pockets and yet holding an enormous bill imprinted by a stamp that says PAID IN FULL.

We can't repay. But we can be grateful. Who wouldn't be? Grace is unmerited, undeserved, and unearned favor from God. That definition is a good start. And yet we've just begun to explore and discover the wonders of *charis*. Let's continue.

CHAPTER 6

AMAZINGLY IMMUTABLE

"Read my lips. No new taxes."

That famous line from American political history is a promise George H. W. Bush made in his 1988 Republican National Convention speech accepting his party's nomination for president of the United States. Mr. Bush had made opposition to tax increases a centerpiece of his campaign to succeed Ronald Reagan. He went on to win election to the White House, but like many presidents before him, he discovered that, once in office, keeping promises isn't always easy.

In 1990, with both houses of Congress in the hands of the opposition party, Bush ultimately signed into law a compromise tax bill that did increase taxes in several areas. Two years later, candidate Bill Clinton consistently mentioned Bush's broken pledge in his campaign speeches. Mr. Clinton's television ads relentlessly featured clips of Bush's convention "Read my lips" promise juxtaposed with his signing of the tax bill. The strategy worked and "Bush 41" joined the very short list of sitting presidents who did not win reelection.

We generally don't like it when our leaders say one thing and do another. Nevertheless, leaders in the realms of politics and business change their minds all the time. They have to. They're human. They make mistakes. They never have all the information. They certainly don't know the future. Perhaps that's why we sometimes assume God is the same way. But God isn't human, doesn't make mistakes, has all the information, and *does* know the future.

That's why one of the key attributes of our heavenly Father is His *immutability*. That's a fancy word that simply means "unchanging and unchangeable."

It's a word we find in the sixth chapter of Hebrews:

> Thus God, determining to show more abundantly to the heirs of promise the *immutability* of His counsel, confirmed it by an oath, that by two *immutable* things, in which it is impossible for God to lie, we might have strong consolation, who have fled for refuge to lay hold of the hope set before us. (Hebrews 6:17–18, emphasis added)

Again, the word *immutable*, and its relative *immutability*, simply mean "unchanging and unchangeable." That's the meaning of the Greek word *ametathetos*, which is translated "immutability" in that verse. In fact, several other translations use the word *unchangeable* there. *Ametathetos* means "fixed"..."unmoving and unmovable." These two appearances in this passage are the only places they appear in the entire Bible.

When you look at the word *immutable*, if you squint, you can see the root of another couple of words embedded there. I'm talking about the root of the words *mutate* or *mutation*. Those words refer to a process of change. Of course, the prefix *im* means "not." The *im* turns the word *possible* into *impossible* and the word *movable* into *immovable*. In the same way, the prefix *im* turns something that can be mutated or changed into something that cannot change.

These verses in Hebrews 6, as well as a good number of other verses in your Bible, bring us an important, comforting truth. God cannot change. He has no need to change because He's perfect. He is immutable and as a result, so are his promises and decrees. George H. W. Bush was, in my view, a good and decent man. Yet he, and every other leader in human history, being human, had changes of mind and broke some promises. Contrast that with the declaration of Numbers 23:19: "God is not a man, that he should lie, nor son of man, that he should repent." Or 1 Samuel 15:29: "And also the Strength of Israel will not lie nor relent. For He is not a man, that He should relent." The word *Strength* is capitalized there because this verse is clearly talking about God. Or how about Malachi 3:6: "For I am the Lord, I do not change." Or Titus 1:2: "In hope of eternal life which God, who cannot lie, promised before time began."

I suspect you're beginning to get the picture. God doesn't change. He doesn't change his mind. He can't lie. Most Christians would look at that statement and say, "Of course! I know that!" And yet...

Many believers don't transfer this conviction to their understanding of grace. They may not be fully aware of it, but in reality, they think God somehow changes His mind about grace once they're saved. They fully and completely know that God *saved* them by grace. But they assume that God's grace steps back into the shadows as they "live the Christian life."

Their paradigm is that their ticket into the theme park called The Kingdom of God was fully paid as a gift, but once inside the park, there is a cashier at each ride with his hand out, demanding that they pay the required fee to go on the ride.

You have to be in the silver-haired demographic, as I am (barely!), to remember when Disneyland operated on a ticket-book system. Today, you pay one price at the gate and ride anything you want as many times as you're willing to wait in line. But that wasn't always the case. When I was young, Disneyland had a different system. At the gate you purchased a book of tickets. Those tickets were designated with a letter—A through E. An A ticket got you into the stuff no kid ever wanted to do or see.

> Their paradigm is that their ticket into the theme park called The Kingdom of God was fully paid as a gift, but once inside the park, there is a cashier at each ride with his hand out, demanding that they pay the required fee to go on the ride.

Things like the educational exhibits. The B, C, and D tickets got you into progressively more exciting rides. But the very best rides—the big roller coasters and thrill rides—required an E ticket. And once your E tickets were gone, that was it unless you bought more. It was a pay-as-you-go arrangement. That's precisely how a tragically large number of believers think about their lives in God. They might not frame it in these terms in their thinking, but in reality, they've been taught that the Christian life is pay-as-you-go.

This, by the way, is how you end up with metaphors about oars and rowing required to earn access to God or get to heaven. And at the root of all this thinking is an assumption that God changes the arrangement after you're saved. That grace gets you into the foyer of the house, but after that you have to earn your place at the table. But that is not the testimony of God's Word.

Have you ever noticed Paul's exhortation in Colossians 2:6?

As you therefore have received Christ Jesus the Lord, so walk in Him.

It's a short sentence with a big message, with huge implications. The Holy Spirit, through Paul, is telling the believers at Colossae how to live the Christian life. How? The same way you started it. And how did they start it? According to Ephesians 2:8–9, "by grace...through faith, and that not of yourselves; it is the gift of God, not of works, lest anyone should boast." In other words, God doesn't change systems after you are born again. The way we get into Christ is the same way we live in Him.

This becomes even clearer in the verses that immediately follow Colossians 2:6. Here's verse 7:

...rooted and built up in Him and established in the faith, as you have been taught, abounding in it with thanksgiving.

God's gift of salvation by grace caused us to be rooted "in Him [Jesus]" and then built up "in Him." This results in abounding in "thanksgiving." Do you recall the patron-client system from chapter 4, through which the Greek concept of *charis* originated? Do you recall what the obligation of the client who received *charis* from a patron was in that system? Gratitude! Or in Paul's word, thanksgiving. Receiving the *charis* gift of salvation does something in our lives. Grace naturally, organically produces certain effects in our lives because we're firmly rooted and built up in Jesus. And that process continues throughout our lives in God, if we'll avoid being moved out of that posture of humble gratitude. Paul addresses this danger in the very next verse:

Beware lest anyone cheat you through philosophy and empty deceit, according to the tradition of men, according to the basic principles of the world, and not according to Christ. For in Him dwells all the fullness of the Godhead bodily; and *you are complete in Him*, who is the head of all principality and power. (Colossians 2:8–10, emphasis added)

A philosophy or theology that pulls you away from grateful receiving in grace cheats you, Paul says. The truth is, in Him, we are complete. We're enough.

> A philosophy or theology that pulls you away from grateful receiving in grace cheats you, Paul says. The truth is, in Him, we are complete. We're enough.

This isn't the only place in the New Testament we receive this encouragement to stay in grace through faith. Or put another way, to continue to have faith in God's grace. The entire book of Galatians is a letter from Paul to a group of people who were being seduced away from grace and back into the lifeless system of rule following, Law keeping, and trying to pay back. Note Paul's stern and frantic warning in the opening verses of Galatians, Chapter 3:

O foolish Galatians! Who has bewitched you that you should not obey the truth, before whose eyes Jesus Christ was clearly portrayed among you as crucified? This only I want to learn from you: Did you receive the Spirit by the works of the law, or by the hearing of faith? Are you so foolish? Having begun in the Spirit, are you now being made perfect by the flesh? Have you suffered so many things in vain—if indeed it was in vain? Therefore He who supplies the Spirit to you and works

42

miracles among you, does He do it by the works of the law, or by the hearing of faith? (v. 1–5)

Here Paul echoes the same truth he delivered to the Colossians. Namely, that you continue the Christian life the same way you began it. That is, in a humble willingness to receive grace! He says, paraphrasing the passage you just read:

Guys! Did you receive the gift of the Holy Spirit—that is, get saved and filled with the Spirit—by grace or by doing something to earn it? Have you really become so foolish as to think that what could only have begun by the Spirit, you're now going to continue in your own strength? Really, guys? When that same Spirit does miracles among you, is it because you've earned and deserved them? Or are they gracious gifts from a gracious Giver by His Spirit?

No, we continue our journey in God the same way we began it. By being humble enough to admit we're broke. That we're standing at the college registrar's window with loose change in our pockets facing a bill of thousands of dollars.

> We forget that grace is the pure undefiled, unmerited, unearned, undeserved favor of God toward sinful, spiritually bankrupt people.

This truth gets confused a lot in the body of Christ. We forget that grace is the pure undefiled, unmerited, unearned, undeserved favor of God toward sinful, spiritually bankrupt people. That we need it as much today as we did the day we were saved. That God's way of dealing with us doesn't *mutate* into something different on Day 2 of our born-again journey. Why? Because God and His ways are *immutable.*

A couple of chapters later in Galatians, Dr. Paul writes us the prescription for curing the "foolishness" of wandering away from God's gracious system:

> Stand fast therefore in the liberty by which Christ has made us free, and do not be entangled again with a yoke of bondage. (Galatians 5:1)

Do you see the contrast? On one hand there is a life of "the liberty by which Christ has made us free." The alternative is being "entangled again with a yoke of bondage." A few verses later, Dr. Paul gives a grim diagnosis for those who have fully fallen back into the fruitless, frustrating system of trying to merit, deserve, and earn:

> You have become estranged from Christ, you who attempt to be justified by law; you have fallen from grace. (Galatians 5:4)

Please note: *Estranged* does not mean "divorced." Many have interpreted the phrase *fallen from grace* to mean a person is no longer saved or connected to God. That's not the message here. A spouse that has chosen to sleep on the couch is estranged, but still very much married.

God is immutable. So are His ways. And in this new system established and sealed by the blood of Jesus through His sacrificial death on the cross, His outreach and adoption of us through grace is immutable, too. This new system is literally a new *covenant.* By the way, God has always chosen to engage, help, and bless humanity through the vehicle of covenant. We see covenants with Adam, Noah, Abraham, Israel, and numerous other groups of people. We're going to explore the concept of covenant more thoroughly in the next chapter, but for now just know that this is why we began this chapter in Hebrews—the New Testament book that most clearly spells out how the New Covenant, made possible by Jesus' life and sacrificial death, is distinct and different from the Old Covenant. For now, just note that when I talk about the Old Covenant I'm referring to the covenant through which God made the Israelite tribes into a distinct people with a special role to play in His plan to redeem the whole world. (Because it was mediated by Moses, it's sometimes called the Mosaic Covenant.)

We'll be visiting the book of Hebrews quite a bit in the chapters ahead. But for now, let's close the loop, return to Hebrews Chapter 6, and unpack the verse with which we began:

> Thus God, determining to show more abundantly to the heirs of promise the *immutability* of His counsel, confirmed it by an oath, that by two *immutable* things, in which it is impossible for God to lie, we might have strong consolation, who have fled for refuge to lay hold of the hope set before us. (Hebrews 6:17–18, emphasis added)

The "heirs of promise" referenced here are you, and me, and every other person living or dead who at one time said yes to God's gracious offer to be their patron and received His abundant *charis* gift. This entire passage is talking about God's extravagant promises to Abraham. Promises wrapped in the solemn, unbreakable vehicle of covenant. (The Abrahamic Covenant, as it is known.) And as Paul reveals in Galatians, everyone who is "in Christ"—that is, every believer—is an heir to all of the promises made to Abraham (see Galatians 3:15–29). And we know God will be faithful to those promises because He is immutable. He cannot lie. So this produces hope… "the hope set before us." With that in mind look at the next verse:

This hope we have as an anchor of the soul, both sure and steadfast… (Hebrews 6:19a)

"This hope…" What hope is "this" referring to? The hope that God will not change His mind about any of the "exceedingly great and precious promises" (2 Peter 1:4) that make up the New Covenant. We're going to take a much deeper dive into those New Covenant promises in the next part. But for now I just want to put a spotlight on what this hope does. It becomes "an anchor of the soul, both sure and steadfast."

Boating has been a significant part of my life the last few decades, so I know a thing or two about anchors. In fact, I humbly consider myself a minor authority on the art and science of anchoring. I speak from experience when I tell you that "sure and steadfast" are very good things when it comes to anchors.

The initial recipients and readers of the letter that became our biblical book called Hebrews were Jewish Christians living in the middle of a time of intense persecution and convulsive change. To these messianic believers in Jesus, it had to seem as if their whole world was capsizing. Storms of trouble and change were raging all around them. *This* is the context of the writer's words in Hebrews 6:17–18 about an "immutable" God not being capable of lying. And in that knowledge, they "who have fled for refuge" to Him should take "strong consolation" in that knowledge and "lay hold of the hope set before us."

It was that hope in a faithful God's immutable promise keeping that those believers could have a "sure and steadfast" anchor for their souls. That anchor remains available for you and me. This "anchor" metaphor rings so true to me. Invariably after a hurricane, we see photographs of heavily damaged boats blown or swept onto dry land. That is often the sign of anchoring that was neither sure nor steadfast. When we anchor our souls (our minds, wills, and emotions) in the hope that comes from knowing God is unchanging and keeps His promises, we come through even the most ferocious of life's storms.

> Everything about God is immutable, including His grace.

Everything about God is immutable, including His grace. He doesn't begin His relationship with you on the basis of grace and then change systems on you. We just took note of Paul's exasperated question to the believers in Galatia who seemed to have been confused on that point. He asked:

> Did you receive the Spirit by the works of the law, or by the hearing of faith? Are you so foolish? Having begun in the Spirit, are you now being made perfect by the flesh? (Galatians 3:3)

Today, Paul could ask the same question to many believers who are frantically trying to row their way to heaven, or at least into God's favor. So many fall into the trap of believing that they got their start by grace but are now supposed to get the rest of the way with striving, straining, and struggling—that is, earning, meriting, and deserving.

No, God is covenantal. And the New Covenant begins and ends with our immutable God's immutable grace. That New Covenant is extraordinary. It is good news in every imaginable sense of that term. So we should explore it, don't you think?

PART 2

NEW AND BETTER, PERIOD.

CHAPTER 7

A NEW AND BETTER COVENANT

They didn't see it coming. None of them.

Not the Pharisees and their obsessive, meticulous parsing of the Law and the Prophets in the synagogues. Not the Sadducees with their elite educations and access to the greatest Jewish minds of their time. Neither did the Levites ministering in Herod's Temple every day with the High Priest as their leader. It just wasn't on their radar. Equally unaware were the seventy-two members of the Great Sanhedrin—Judaism's equivalent to our Supreme Court—who met each day in a building at the Temple complex called the Hall of Hewn Stones.

None of them, even with the benefit of accumulated centuries of poring over the Scriptures, seemed to have expected the Messiah to do what Jesus actually did when He arrived.

Yes, they were expecting the Messiah. In fact, at the time Jesus came on the scene, their long-simmering expectation was already at a rolling boil. But the prevailing expectation was that the Messiah would be a David-like champion and enforcer of God's fifteen-hundred-year-old Mosaic Covenant with Israel.

Not the bringer of a new one.

A new covenant with God's special people? That was simply unthinkable. But it shouldn't have been. It was right there in the book of the prophet Jeremiah in plain and unambiguous language:

"Behold, the days are coming, says the LORD, when I will make *a new covenant* with the house of Israel and with the house of Judah—not according to the covenant that I made with their fathers in the day that I took them by the hand to lead them out of the land of Egypt, My covenant which they broke, though I was a husband to them, says the LORD. But this is the covenant that I will make with the house of Israel after those days, says the LORD: I will put My law in their minds, and write it on their hearts; and I will be their God, and they shall be My people. No more shall every man teach his neighbor, and every man his brother, saying, 'Know the LORD,' for they all shall know Me, from the least of them to the greatest of them, says the LORD. For I will forgive their iniquity, and their sin I will remember no more." (Jeremiah 31:31–34, emphasis added)

A "new covenant." God spoke this prophecy through Jeremiah roughly six hundred years before the birth of Jesus. And this coming covenant will not just be "new," said the prophecy, but also *different* from the one God had made with the Israelites immediately after delivering them from bondage in Egypt. The New King James says that this new covenant is "*not according* to the covenant that I made with their fathers..." But other translations are clearer.

Young's Literal Translation, the New American Standard, the Tree of Life Version (a Messianic Jewish translation), and numerous other respected translations all say that this new covenant will be "not like" the covenant God made with their forefathers. In other words, the covenant that Jeremiah foresaw God making "with the house of Judah and the house of Israel" would be a different *kind* of covenant than they had previously known. As we'll see as we continue this journey, this is such an important key to understanding grace!

There are several things that are vital to understand. Again, God has always chosen to work with humanity through covenant. It's just His way. This use of covenants reveals that there is a legal or judicial order in God's way of doing things. God is not chaotic or capricious. He is not an outlaw. On the contrary, He brings order out of chaos. And to support that order He framed the universe with a certain set of laws and principles that, in His righteousness and holiness, He cannot violate. (Remember God's immutability. He cannot change!)

This helps us understand why God operates through covenant. A covenant is a sacred legal agreement between parties. But as Jeremiah's prophecy suggests and as you're about to see, there is more than one kind of covenant.

> God has always chosen to work with humanity through covenant. It's just His way.

As I mentioned in the previous chapter, God made covenantal arrangements with Adam and Eve, with Noah, and with Abraham. Then, when it came time for God to have a covenant people on the earth again, He picked Moses to be the mediator of His covenant with the Israelites. Now hang with me here for a bit while I give you a short history lesson that will be super beneficial to your understanding of just how truly amazing God's grace is.

Our gracious God always meets us where we are and speaks in terms we can understand. He speaks our language rather than demanding that we learn His. I mention this because when it came time to make a covenant with the Israelites, God picked a form of covenant that they, especially Moses, a prince of Egypt, would have already been familiar with.

> Our gracious God always meets us where we are and speaks in terms we can understand.

Here's where I need you to stick with me. This gets so good! In the ancient world of the Bible, there were basically two kinds of covenants or treaties between the kings of nations or heads of tribes. The first is called a suzerain-vassal treaty. The second is called a parity treaty.

Suzerain is just a fancy word describing a very powerful king who is in a dominant position over other neighboring kings. In ancient times a stronger king might go to one of his weaker neighbors (the prospective vassal) and say something along these lines:

Look, we both know I could squash you like a bug. I could come in here with my vast armies, destroy all the cities, wipe out your armies, kill you, and take over your country. But then what good is it to me? I would have a new chunk of land with destroyed cities to have to govern. Here's another option. Let's draft a treaty where you promise to be loyal to me, pay me an annual tribute that symbolizes that loyalty, and you lend me some of your soldiers if I need them. In return, not only will I not destroy you, but I'll actually protect you if you're attacked. Which option do you choose?

These kinds of treaties were very common in the ancient Near East. Archaeologists have dug up scores of them carved into stone or pressed into clay tablets. The Old Testament mentions them in numerous places, too. Take 2 Kings 17:3, for example:

Shalmaneser king of Assyria came up against him; and Hoshea became his vassal, and paid him tribute money.

Here's another one:

In his days Nebuchadnezzar king of Babylon came up, and Jehoiakim became his vassal for three years. (2 Kings 24:1)

The terms of these suzerain-vassal covenants were always spelled out in detail in treaty documents that had a common structure. Keep that in mind. But as I mentioned, there was another common form of covenant between kings or tribal leaders in that era of history.

The parity covenant was a treaty between two kings of relatively equal power and status. This is a covenant in which two leaders or kings come together and pledge loyalty to each other. Each says to the other something along these lines:

If you are attacked, I'll consider that an attack on me and come to your defense. If you have a need, I'll supply it if I can. What is mine is yours. We are now family.

This involved something called cutting covenant, because the two parties might cut themselves on their palms or wrists and then clasp hands, causing their blood to intermingle. (Attention 1970s movie buffs: There's a great scene at the end of the movie *The Outlaw Josey Wales* in which Clint Eastwood's character does this very thing with the chief of a nearby Indian tribe.) Again, this kind of covenant made two separate families or peoples "one." The ceremony also sometimes included cutting one or more animals in half. The two parties would walk between the halved animal carcasses while swearing, "May this or worse happen to me if I ever violate my faithfulness to this covenant." (More on this later!) Such a covenant was usually sealed with a symbolic exchange of items—often rings and/or robes—and culminated with a meal. As you can now see, another good name for a parity covenant would be peer-to-peer.

I took the time to explain all of this because it directly relates to Jeremiah's prophecy about the "new covenant" God would one day make with the houses of Judah and Israel. His prophecy revealed that this covenant would be a different kind than the one God made with the Israelites through Moses. And what many people don't understand is that the Mosaic Covenant was based on the suzerain-vassal model!

Many biblical scholars have pointed out that the whole structure of the book of Deuteronomy—the book of the Bible in which the terms of God's covenant with the Israelites are most fully spelled out—closely matches the structure of those ancient suzerain-vassal treaty documents. That's no accident. God chose this form of covenant for a couple of reasons.

First, as I mentioned previously, as the adopted son of Pharaoh, Moses would have been intimately acquainted with the suzerain-vassal treaty concept. Egypt, as a world power, had crafted this type of treaty with weaker nations many times. Moses would have had a front-row seat for such negotiations and treaty signings.

Second, God chose this form of covenant because the other form—the parity covenant—simply wasn't available to Him. Not yet anyway. To make a peer-to-peer treaty, you have to have a peer in the other tribe—someone of comparable power and status—with whom to cut covenant. At that point in redemptive history there was no human on earth who could stand face-to-face with God as a peer. So instead, God chose to make the Israelite people His special "vassal." The short form of the treaty was carved on tablets of stone, front and back. There were two tablets because when a contract of covenant is signed, both parties get a copy of the document (see Exodus 31:18). The long form of the covenant is the book of Deuteronomy.

Now, there is one more thing you need to know about the suzerain-vassal form of covenant: It's a *conditional* agreement. In other words, all the blessings and protections the suzerain agrees to provide for the vassal are conditioned upon the vassal remaining loyal and faithful to the agreement. If the vassal violates the covenant, the suzerain is released from his obligations under the agreement. So the super-powerful king comes to the weak vassal and offers a series of "if...then" promises: "If you will do X...then I will do Y." If...then!

The books of Exodus, Numbers, and Deuteronomy are chock-full of examples of God framing promises to Israel in just those terms. It's a fascinating and illuminating exercise to go through the Old Testament and find all the places God told Israel, "If you will do X, then I will do Y."

One of the most well known of these is 2 Chronicles 7:14:

If My people who are called by My name will humble themselves, and pray and seek My face, and turn from their wicked ways, *then* I will hear from heaven, and will forgive their sin and heal their land. (emphasis added)

In the twenty-eighth chapter of Deuteronomy, God is basically summarizing the terms and implications of the suzerain-vassal relationship he had just established through Moses. That chapter starts with these words:

> "*If* you fully obey the LORD your God and carefully keep all his commands that I am giving you today, *[then]* the LORD your God will set you high above all the nations of the world." (Deuteronomy 28:1 NLT, addition mine)

When a New Testament verse or passage explains what an Old Testament passage meant, we should probably believe it, don't you think?

"If... then." This aspect of the suzerain-vassal type of covenant explains why God was legally free to one day speak to a prophet named Jeremiah about a new covenant. A different kind of covenant... *if* the terms of the old one had been repeatedly violated. And they had.

Here is great news. We don't have to wonder about what Jeremiah's prophecy meant. We have New Testament Scriptures that make it very clear. By the way, the most reliable interpreter of the Old Testament is the New Testament. When a New Testament verse or passage explains what an Old Testament passage meant, we should probably believe it, don't you think? And we should do so even when that interpretation surprises us or doesn't fit our preconceived theological notions. We should start with Hebrews Chapter 8, which quotes Jeremiah's prophecy word for word. But first it says this concerning Jesus.

> But now He has obtained a more excellent ministry, inasmuch as He is also *Mediator of a better covenant, which was established on better promises.* For if that first covenant had

been faultless, then no place would have been sought for a second. (Hebrews 8:6–7, emphasis added)

Whereas Moses was the mediator of the Old Covenant, we learn here that the New Covenant's mediator is Jesus himself. Notice also that the new covenant Jesus mediated for us is "better" than the old one and it is established on "better promises." And also notice that the Old covenant wasn't faultless. It had some flaws or defects that kept it from accomplishing what God ultimately intended (which is restoring mankind back to intimate fellowship with Himself). After delivering this new and better revelation, the author of Hebrews anticipates his Jewish readers asking the question: "Why?!"

That is why the writer begins the next sentence with "Because..." and then proceeds to quote all of Jeremiah's prophecy:

Because finding fault with them, He says: "Behold, the days are coming, says the LORD, when I will make a new covenant with the house of Israel and with the house of Judah—not according to the covenant that I made with their fathers in the day when I took them by the hand to lead them out of the land of Egypt; *because they did not continue in My covenant*, and I disregarded them, says the LORD. For this is the covenant that I will make with the house of Israel after those days, says the LORD: I will put My laws in their mind and write them on their hearts; and I will be their God, and they shall be My people. None of them shall teach his neighbor, and none his brother, saying, 'Know the LORD,' for all shall know Me, from the least of them to the greatest of them. *For I will be merciful to their unrighteousness, and their sins and their lawless deeds I will remember no more.*" (Hebrews 8:8–12, emphasis added)

So what are the implications of the arrival of this new covenant based on better promises? What is Jesus' role in it? And what does any of this have to do with grace?

Answers to all those questions and more lie on the pages that follow. Spoiler alert: Good news up ahead!

CHAPTER 8

NEW AND BETTER VERSUS OBSOLETE AND VANISHING

My apologies in advance for the graphic illustration, but people who grew up on a farm a couple of generations ago knew well that you can cut the head off a chicken and it will still run around the barnyard for a while. But ultimately, the thing will fall over so it can end up breaded and in a frying pan.

An airplane in flight can lose all engine power and still glide for a while. But eventually gravity will do what gravity does.

My point is that there are many examples in life of things that have effectively died but still continue for a while. I'm reminded of that reality whenever I read the book of Hebrews. It is a book written in an in-between time. A time in which the Mosaic Covenant—with its system of 613 laws and regulations and all of the Temple rites and rituals—had been rendered obsolete because Jesus had completely fulfilled them (see Matthew 5:17–18), and yet the covenant was still gliding along.

As the book's name suggests, Hebrews was written to Jewish

people. The exact identity of the author is unknown, but the theology of the book is very Paul-ish. So if it wasn't written personally by Paul, it was certainly penned by someone who had been profoundly influenced by Paul's direct and personal revelation of Jesus and Jesus' mission. Scholars generally place the writing of this letter in the mid-60s, that is, around A.D. 65 or 66.

In other words, at the time of the writing it had been roughly three and a half decades since Jesus ascended to heaven and then, ten days later, poured out the Holy Spirit onto 120 of His followers on the Day of Pentecost. The first Holy Spirit–anointed sermon had been preached on that momentous day, as Peter, accompanied by a handful of other freshly fire-baptized disciples, stepped out of the upper room and began to speak. Three thousand Jewish people from points all over the known world heard and responded to a brand-new message. That message was that Jesus of Nazareth was the fulfillment of everything the Law and the Prophets had been pointing to through the Old Testament Scriptures. The risen Jesus said so, Himself.

> Then He said to [the disciples], "These are the words which I spoke to you while I was still with you, that all things must be fulfilled which were written in the Law of Moses and the Prophets and the Psalms concerning Me." And He opened their understanding, that they might comprehend the Scriptures. (Luke 24:44–45, addition mine)

Jesus said these things just before His ascension into heaven. So it's not surprising that this became the message of the disciples as they took the famous Roman roads to tell their fellow Jews that the Messiah had come and, just as the Old Covenant Scriptures foretold, had suffered; had died a sacrificial, atoning death; and had risen to the right hand of the Father in heaven.

The disciples and their converts had gone to wherever there were Jewish communities, preaching in their synagogues and market-places. Even Paul, the self-proclaimed "apostle to the Gentiles," made the local synagogue his very first stop whenever entering a new city. Why? He answers that question in Romans 1:16:

> For I am not ashamed of the gospel of Christ, for it is the power of God to salvation for everyone who believes, *for the Jew first* and also for the Greek. (emphasis added)

As a result, in the months, years, and decades that followed the Day of Pentecost outpouring, Jewish people by the hundreds of thousands became Jesus followers. Communities of believing Jews sprang up everywhere, but the oldest, largest, and most influential of the messianic congregations was in the mother city, Jerusalem— the place it all began. Thus, it is believed by some that the letter we call Hebrews was written from a Church leader in Rome to the Jewish believers in Jerusalem, but with predominantly Jewish congregations everywhere in mind.

The content of the letter also assumes that those congregations had in attendance Jewish people who had not yet fully committed. People who were curious, intrigued about Jesus, drawn to the miracles, attracted by the love of the brothers and sisters—and yet had not authentically surrendered their hearts and lives. In a sense, they had one foot in the New Covenant and one foot in the old one. The book of Hebrews contains several stark, sobering warnings to such people.

With just a little historical context, we can understand why many were reluctant to embrace Jesus as Messiah, surrender to Him, and join the Jesus movement. The book of Hebrews was written in a time of intense pressure on and persecution of the infant Church. That persecution was coming from two places.

First, from the very beginning the Jewish establishment in Jerusalem had opposed the Jesus movement and persecuted it. Before long, that program was extended beyond Jerusalem to wherever the disciples of Jesus traveled to share their faith in the synagogues. Paul himself encountered this counter-movement in numerous cities after his Damascus road conversion. He was nearly beaten to death on numerous occasions. But this wasn't the only source of pressure on the young Church of Jesus Christ.

> By the 60s, the likely time of the writing of the book of Hebrews, the fledgling Church was facing persecution from a second source—the Roman Empire.

By the 60s, the likely time of the writing of the book of Hebrews, the fledgling Church was facing persecution from a second source—the Roman Empire.

All of this meant that for any Jewish person thinking about professing faith in Jesus Christ, it was no casual decision. On the one hand he or she would likely be, at best, disowned by both family and community. On the other, it meant possibly facing imprisonment, torture, and death at the hands of the Romans.

In the light of what you now know, this familiar exhortation takes on fresh meaning:

> And let us consider one another in order to stir up love
> and good works, not forsaking the assembling of ourselves

together, as is the manner of some, but exhorting one another, and so much the more as you see the Day approaching. (Hebrews 10:24–25)

That "Day" was the rapidly approaching fulfillment of what Jesus had prophesied and what His disciples had been preaching all over the known world. That is, a judgment upon Jerusalem that would bring a once-and-for-all end to the sacrificial system at the heart of the Old Covenant. This explains why Hebrews is also filled with dire warnings to Jewish readers who were hanging around the fringes of the Jesus people assemblies but hadn't yet committed and surrendered. Those warnings include this one, which makes reference to the unbelieving Israelites who refused to enter the Promised Land:

Therefore, since a promise remains of entering His rest, let us fear lest any of you seem to have come short of it. For indeed the gospel was preached to us as well as to them; but the word which they heard did not profit them, not being mixed with faith in those who heard it. (Hebrews 4:1–2)

All of this is why I mentioned earlier that Hebrews was written and circulated during an in-between time where the two great covenants were concerned. *Overlap* is probably a better term. Jesus had famously predicted the destruction of the Jerusalem Temple. But now more than three decades had passed and nothing had happened. The Temple rituals were still going on, day after day, year after year. The annual Day of Atonement and Passover sacrifices—the ones Jesus' disciples kept claiming had pointed to Him and His sacrificial death—were still being offered up on the hill in Herod's magnificent Temple. "How could Jesus have fulfilled these if they were still going on?" the skeptics argued.

For many Jesus followers, this was a problem. For many opponents of the new Jesus movement, it seemed to be evidence that Jesus' claims were false. Recall that one of the statements the Jewish elites used to accuse Jesus centered on His statement that not one stone of the Temple would be left upon another (see Matthew 24:2, Luke 21:6). Both Jesus and John the Baptist had warned of a coming judgment. But at the time that book of Hebrews was written, nothing had happened.

What few if any understood at the time of Hebrews' writing was that Jesus' prophecy was only four or five years away from being completely fulfilled. On the eve of Passover, A.D. 70—essentially forty years to the day after Jesus' crucifixion—Roman armies began encircling Jerusalem. Jesus had warned his followers that this was the sign to immediately flee the city and escape to the Judean hills, which, Church history testifies, they did. The armies of General Titus besieged the city and ultimately breached her walls. Before they were finished, what Jesus had prophesied had been completely and utterly fulfilled.

Now you understand why I opened this chapter with the mention of the proverbial headless chicken and a powerless airplane still gliding on momentum. The arrival of the New Covenant ended the need for the old one. But the old one had continued to glide for several decades. The book of Hebrews is the New Testament's clearest and most detailed explanation of the relationship between the Old and New Covenants.

> The arrival of the New Covenant ended the need for the old one.

And you can't begin to comprehend grace without this understanding.

The Old Covenant, with Moses as the mediator, had been enacted in a season that began with the first Passover and culminated fifty days later with the giving of the Law on Mount Sinai.

The New Covenant, with Jesus as the mediator, had been enacted in a season that began with Jesus' Passover Eve death on Mount Zion and culminated fifty days later with the outpouring of the Holy Spirit on the Day of Pentecost.

That Old Covenant involved laws written on tablets of stone. But the New Covenant's requirements were instead written upon each individual heart.

As we've seen, that revelation had been embedded in Jeremiah Chapter 31 for centuries. And it is quoted at length in Hebrews Chapter 8. There, the Bible makes it abundantly clear that Jesus, and the new way of living in God that He ushered in, was and is the fulfillment of Jeremiah's prophecy. We also read Hebrews 8:6, which declared that the new was a "better covenant... established on better promises."

All of that was remarkable enough. But, continuing to illuminate Jeremiah's prophecy, the writer of Hebrews drops the true bombshell a few verses later. In the final verse of Chapter 8 we see:

In that He says, "A new covenant," He has made the first obsolete. Now what is becoming obsolete and growing old is ready to vanish away. (Hebrews 8:13)

Do you see it? The new makes the old "obsolete." And to make sure we don't miss the implications of that statement, the writer graciously spells it out for us. Remember, this is being written in the overlap period between the two covenants. The moment Jesus poured out the Holy Spirit on the Day of Pentecost—writing the good-news terms of His New Covenant on born-again hearts—the old one was rendered completely obsolete. And what is obsolete, the writer informs us, is "growing old" and is about to "vanish." And he was right!

But why? That mystery solved just ahead.

CHAPTER 9

WHY A NEW COVENANT?

Upgrade. For people who travel frequently, it may be the single sweetest word in the English lexicon. Whether it's a flight, a rental car, or a hotel room, an upgrade is never a bad thing. In other words, it's *good news*.

I'm sure I don't have to tell you that everything God does is good. He doesn't make mistakes. He never does something and suddenly thinks of a better idea. So in the light of what we've been seeing, that presents some questions.

How can we explain the fact that roughly fifteen hundred years after crafting and instituting a meticulously detailed covenant with the Israelites, God introduced a better covenant into the timeline of history? How could God upgrade something He Himself had done? And if there was a better kind of covenant, why didn't God put *that* kind in place to begin with? You're about to learn the answer to those questions.

In the previous two chapters we learned that Jesus ushered in a new and better covenant than the one established with the Israelites through Moses. A different *kind* of covenant. We saw that the original covenant was built on the suzerain-vassal model of a treaty between kings or nations. This type of covenant was a *conditional* (if...then) agreement. In this model, the powerful partner, the suzerain or lord, gave the vassal a list of rules to follow. And *if* the vassal faithfully followed those rules, the suzerain would *then* provide protection, provision, and other blessings. But if the vassal violated the requirements of the treaty (the stipulations or laws), the treaty called for serious punishments (sanctions). And if the vassal continued to violate the stipulations and rebel, the suzerain might terminate the covenant completely. This, again, made that kind of covenant a conditional one.

We also saw earlier that the New Covenant, established and mediated by Jesus, was built on a different model. A parity covenant is between two peers who pledge mutual loyalty and support to each other. The two parties of a parity covenant are peers, or equals, who say to each other, unconditionally:

Whatever I have is available to you. What's mine is yours.
If you're attacked, I consider it an attack on me.
We're family. We're one.

Perhaps you are now beginning to see why this was not the first type of covenant God instituted. Remember, a parity covenant is between peers. If you are the head of a tribe and you want to establish such a covenant with another tribe, you have to have a peer in that other tribe. Our "tribe" was humanity. Lost, broken, sin-defiled humanity. Where was God going to find a peer among us? There wasn't one! That meant the better parity covenant wasn't available to Him. Not yet, anyway!

Nevertheless, from the very beginning, from the very day of

the Fall of mankind in the garden, God had a plan for restoring us to intimate fellowship with Him. The Old Covenant didn't heal the terrible wound sin had inflicted—that is, the loss of intimate relationship with the Creator. It could, at best, only serve as a big, annual Band-Aid to cover the wound. No, the centerpiece of that plan for complete healing required getting a human peer of God to the earth…a human being who could represent all of humanity in a peer-to-peer covenant with God. So immediately after the Fall, as God is pronouncing the terrible implications of what Adam and Eve have done, He inserts a note of hope. He speaks of a day in which a descendant, or "seed," of the first woman would crush or "bruise" the head of the deceiver-serpent that had instigated this catastrophe. To that serpent, God said:

> And I will make enemies of you and the woman, and of your offspring and her Descendant [seed]; He shall bruise you on the head, and you shall bruise Him on the heel. (Genesis 3:15 NASB, addition mine)

God's words here are significant but intentionally vague. He dared not disclose the full implications of His plan to undo the damage that had been done. What we now know in hindsight is that this promised "Descendant" would be fully human and yet also fully God. One of His names would be Immanuel, which means "God with us."

Yes, Jesus was God's plan from the very beginning. As the book of Hebrews makes clear, Jesus was the

Yes, Jesus was God's plan from the very beginning. As the book of Hebrews makes clear, Jesus was the mediator of the new and better covenant.

mediator of the new and better covenant. Moses had represented the Israelites on Mount Sinai in the forging of that suzerain-vassal covenant with God. And fifteen hundred years later Jesus had represented both Israel *and* all of humanity in the forging of a parity covenant with Him.

This New Covenant was essentially between God the Father and God the Son. The only way you or I or any other fallen, sinful human could be included in it is by being "in" Jesus. That's why the heart of the miracle of the new birth is an individual being baptized into Jesus:

> For as many of you as were baptized into Christ have put on Christ. (Galatians 3:27)
>
> Or do you not know that as many of us as were baptized into Christ Jesus were baptized into His death? (Romans 6:3)
>
> For by one Spirit we were all baptized into one body—whether Jews or Greeks, whether slaves or free—and have all been made to drink into one Spirit. (1 Corinthians 12:13)

Yes, the "new and better" covenant—a covenant that would restore all willing Jews *and* all willing Gentiles to intimate connection with God—was the Father's plan from the very beginning. But the Old Covenant was a necessary bridge to that ultimate one. Without the Old Covenant there could be no human "peer" with whom God could enter into a parity covenant.

Through Moses, God established a people, so those people could produce one Man.

Now the purpose of the Old

Covenant and the people that it created (the Israelites) comes into sharp focus for us. You've likely heard the tribes of Israel described as God's chosen people. That's an accurate biblical designation. But it prompts a question: Chosen for what? Now we know! God needed a people that could serve as the carrier of that seed or Descendant promised to Eve back in the garden. This is why God spoke to Abraham of seeds (plural) and a Seed (singular) that would one day bless all the people of the earth (see Genesis 22:18). It's why all the meticulously prescribed aspects of the Tabernacle and its ceremonies pointed to Jesus.

Think about it. Why would God have asked Abraham to sacrifice his only, miraculously conceived son? Yes, it tested and proved the man's faith in God. But that could have been proven a thousand other ways. Why *that* way? It is because it was seemingly necessary, given the judicial-legal order upon which God has built this universe, that everything in the Old Covenant would not only foreshadow but also *forerun* God's ultimate and complete remedy for the Fall of mankind. That remedy was Jesus with the new, better covenant His sacrificial death would make possible. And it seems that if God was going to create a people who would one day produce God's only begotten Son, so He could offer that Son up as a sacrifice for the sins for the whole world, He had to have as the father of that people a man willing to do the same thing with his own precious son.

We began this chapter with a question in the title: "Why a New Covenant?" Now we know. *The parity covenant of grace that Jesus mediated was God's ultimate plan from the very beginning.* That suzerain-vassal covenant mediated by Moses was a good, very necessary bridge to that ultimate plan. But it was never intended to, nor could it ever, accomplish the goal of restoring lost humanity to a God who "so loved the world."

With this and the previous two chapters as a foundation, we are now ready to embark upon an exciting adventure into grace. An adventure made possible by Jesus and the covenant He ratified with His own guiltless blood. John described this journey into Jesus as receiving grace upon grace (see John 1:16). And as you're about to discover, everything about that covenant is both new and better. Or in other words, an upgrade.

In fact, it begins with getting an upgraded "husband."

"A husband, Robert?"

Yes, read on and discover what I mean!

CHAPTER 10

BY GRACE: A BETTER HUSBAND

It's a time-tested plot gimmick for sitcom and comedy screenplay writers. Two people somehow accidentally get married. Sometimes the inadvertent wedding involves excessive alcohol consumption. Sometimes it's just the result of a big misunderstanding. (Has there ever been a romantic comedy movie plot that *wasn't* built around a "big misunderstanding"?) Of course, sitcoms are not real life, so it's not likely that people routinely wake up hung over one morning to discover they accidentally got married to someone.

Nevertheless, in spiritual terms, every person ever born, you and I included, was, or still is, "married" to someone...or more accurately some*thing*...and doesn't even know it. That's the testimony of a Bible passage we're about to explore.

Now, if you've been a Christian for a while, I suspect you have already encountered the biblical concept of the Church being the Bride of Christ. For example, in Revelation 21:9 the angel says to John: "Come, I will show you the bride, the Lamb's wife." And in Ephesians Chapter 5, Paul ties his advice to husbands and wives to the revelation that earthly marriage depicts the "mystery" of Christ and the Church (see Ephesians 5:32). Which means that every believer who helps make up the Church is, in a very real sense, by grace, married to Christ. And what a wonderful husband He is.

Again, that is widely known. What is less well known is that this marriage to Christ is a *second marriage* for all believers. It's true, as we discover in this passage in Romans:

> Or do you not know, brethren (for I speak to those who know the law), that the law has dominion over a man as long as he lives? For the woman who has a husband is bound by the law to her husband as long as he lives. But if the husband dies, she is released from the law of her husband. So then if, while her husband lives, she marries another man, she will be called an adulteress; but if her husband dies, she is free from that law, so that she is no adulteress, though she has married another man. *Therefore, my brethren, you also have become dead to the law through the body of Christ, that you may be married to another*—to Him who was raised from the dead, that we should bear fruit to God. (Romans 7:1–4, emphasis added)

I'm going to refer back to these verses about death and marriage shortly. But first you need to understand that these four verses lie in the middle of a long section of Romans in which Paul is explaining every believers' relationship to the Law under the New Covenant. Keep in mind that, unlike the book of Hebrews, the book of Romans was *not* primarily addressed to Jewish people. Yes, there were many Jewish believers in Rome, but thousands of Gentile converts to the Jesus movement had been saved, too. And because Christianity was born out of Judaism... because Jesus was the prophesied Jewish Messiah... because all of the Law and the

Prophets and the Psalms pointed to Him...because the New Covenant emerged from the Old...because in its opening decades the movement almost exclusively comprised believing Jews (along with some Gentile "God-fearing ones"—that is, Gentiles who hung out near the synagogues because they had an affinity for Judaism)...for all of these reasons and more...

Gentile Christians had experienced a lot of confusing, conflicting, and just plain wrong teaching about how they were supposed to relate to the Old Testament Law. Paul's entire letter to the Galatians is aimed at combating that kind of confusion and false teaching.

This is the context of Paul's comments in that passage I just quoted. In the previous chapter of Romans, Paul had boldly and clearly declared, "For sin shall not have dominion over you, *for you are not under law but under grace*" (Romans 6:14, emphasis added). Paul had spent much of the previous five chapters of Romans helping believers understand that it had always been faith, not works or Law keeping, that qualified you to be connected to God. He'd pointed out that it was Abraham's faith and not his good behavior that had prompted God to declare him righteous:

> For what does the Scripture say? "Abraham believed God, and it was accounted to him for righteousness." (Romans 4:3)

Another truth comes out in those chapters leading up to Paul's Chapter 7 comment about "husbands" and being "married." It is the revelation that it wasn't just the Israelites who were under the Law. In a very real sense, all of humanity was accountable to God's perfect and eternal standards of holiness and purity. In other words, God's standards of goodness and righteousness weren't only encoded in the Ten Commandments and the rest of the Mosaic regulations and stipulations. No, Paul makes this clear right out of the gate in Romans Chapter 1, where he declares that all people in all places could discern God's pure goodness through the majesty and witness of nature:

> ...just as it is written: "The righteous will live by faith." The wrath of God is being revealed from heaven against all the godlessness and wickedness of people, who suppress the truth by their wickedness, since *what may be known about God is plain to them, because God has made it plain to them. For since the creation of the world God's invisible qualities—his eternal power and divine nature—have been clearly seen, being understood from what has been made, so that people are without excuse.* (Romans 1:17b-20 NIV, emphasis added)

> Yes, long before God carved commandments into tablets of stone for Moses, a form of the Law existed.

Yes, long before God carved commandments into tablets of stone for Moses, a form of the Law existed. The Mosaic Covenant simply encoded it into written form. That's the husband to whom you and I were born married. We've all sinned and fallen far short of God's glory (see Romans 3:23). That means we all are in deep debt to God's immutable holiness and justice.

Now we can understand why Paul spent those four verses in Romans 7 explaining how a spouse is released from all marital obligations if the other spouse dies. Using a natural example that everyone would understand, Paul reveals that our marriage to the Law is nullified by our own death. That "death" occurs when we are born again by being baptized into Christ. Literal water baptism by immersion is an outward picture of an inward reality—one that involves a symbolic burial. Paul says this explicitly in Romans Chapter 6:

> Or do you not know that as many of us as were baptized into Christ Jesus were baptized into His death? *Therefore we were buried with Him through baptism into death*, that just as Christ was raised from the dead by the glory of the Father, even so we also should walk in newness of life. (v. 3–4, emphasis added)

But as Paul points out in that original passage, it's not just that we're released from our original husband. Through the new birth, we're married to a *new* one. Look again: "Therefore, my brethren, you also have become dead to the law through the body of Christ, that you may be married to another..." (Romans 7:4a)

Who is this "another" to whom we're now married? The last half of that verse provides the answer: "...to Him who was raised from the dead, that we should bear fruit to God" (Romans 7:4b).

Please understand. Our ex-husband, the Law, was not bad. On the contrary, the Law—as an expression of God's goodness, righteousness, and holiness—was perfect. No, it wasn't bad, it was just inadequate. It could not restore us to intimate connection to the Father. Nor was that ever the Law's job. So, what *was* and *is* the Law's job? To make us aware that we are sinful, utterly powerless to help ourselves, and in desperate need of a Savior (see Romans 3:20). To make us aware that we had fallen from the place we were originally intended to live—the place of

> Please understand. Our ex-husband, the Law, was not bad...it was just inadequate.

intimate fellowship and communion with our Creator. As Paul told the believers at Corinth, the Law had a ministry...a ministry of death and condemnation:

> But if the *ministry of death,* written and engraved on stones, was glorious, so that the children of Israel could not look steadily at the face of Moses because of the glory of his countenance, which glory was passing away, how will the ministry of the Spirit not be more glorious? For if the *ministry of condemnation* had glory, the ministry of righteousness exceeds much more in glory. (2 Corinthians 3:7–9, emphasis added)

As Paul told the believers at Corinth, the Law had a ministry...a ministry of death and condemnation.

How's that for a job description? "Oh, so you want to go into ministry, Mr. Law? Okay, your ministry will be bringing death and condemnation to everyone, everywhere. Enjoy."

As we see in that passage, our old husband had heavenly glory. This was evidenced by the fact that there was great glory on display when God met with Moses on Mount Sinai, so much so that Moses' face was glowing with it when he came down from the mountain.

Yes, the Law was good and had a ministry, or job, to do. And it did it perfectly! But its job made it a difficult husband to have to live with. Think about it. What kind of husband do you think the Law is? Do you think that he's a forgiving husband? Do you think he is a loving, caring, kind, compassionate, understanding husband? Of course, not. The Law is an overbearing, nitpicky, fault-finding, critical, judgmental husband. A husband you could never please no matter how hard you tried. A husband whose actual ministry to you was one of death and condemnation.

Oh, what an upgrade our new husband is over the old one! And yet many Christians seem to want to go back to living with the first one. Or try to find some way to live with one foot in the old marriage and one in the new. In reality, countless Christians live like polygamists! That is, they seem to have two spiritual husbands.

Here are a few things you, as a reborn believer, need to understand about your "ex."

Number One: The Law cannot justify. From the Fall of mankind forward, no human being was able to stand before God because of our own guilt before the Law. We needed some way to be justified. The Christian doctrine of justification in Jesus Christ is a vital one. Yet the Bible makes it clear that keeping the Law has no ability to justify us in the sight of God. That's the plain-as-day message of these two verses from Romans Chapter 3:

Therefore by the deeds of the law no flesh will be justified in His sight... (v. 20a)
Therefore we conclude that a man is justified by faith apart from the deeds of the law. (v. 28)

And this one as well:

For as many as are of the works of the law are under the curse; for it is written, "Cursed is everyone who does not continue in all things which are written in the book of the law, to do them." But that *no one is justified by the law in the sight of God* is evident, for "the just shall live by faith." (Galatians 3:10–11, emphasis added)

The justification we so desperately require comes only by grace through faith in the Lord Jesus Christ. Yet as we've already seen, Paul had to write the entire book of Galatians to people who were being seduced into going back to that first husband. Which is precisely why Paul wrote these words to them:

> O foolish Galatians! Who has bewitched you that you should not obey the truth, before whose eyes Jesus Christ was clearly portrayed among you as crucified? This only I want to learn from you: *Did you receive the Spirit by the works of the law, or by the hearing of faith?* Are you so foolish? Having begun in the Spirit, are you now being made perfect by the flesh? (Galatians 3:1–3, emphasis added)

I love the way *The Message* paraphrase renders that passage:

> You crazy Galatians! Did someone put a spell on you? Have you taken leave of your senses? Something crazy has happened, for it's obvious that you no longer have the crucified Jesus in clear focus in your lives. His sacrifice on the cross was certainly set before you clearly enough.
>
> Let me put this question to you: How did your new life begin? Was it by working your heads off to please God? Or was it by responding to God's Message to you? Are you going to continue this craziness? For only crazy people would think they could complete by their own efforts what was begun by God.

No, the Law doesn't justify you. It never could, and it never will. But this isn't the only problem with our mutual ex-husband.

Number Two: The Law cannot empower you. The Law cannot give you the ability to do what it relentlessly informs you that you *must* do. It can only tell you what you did wrong. Again. It can only show you how far short you fell. Only bring you back to that same place of shame and fear that had Adam and Eve hiding from God and frantically sewing together fig leaves. Only convince you that you desperately need a sinless Champion, a Righteous Peer of God who can represent you in a Parity Covenant with holy, holy, holy God.

> The Law cannot give you the ability to do what it relentlessly informs you that you *must* do.

Yes, our husband, the Law, had a vital role to play in God's plan to restore us back to Himself, and it played that role perfectly. It still does. But that role does not include giving you the power to change and be fruitful.

Let's revisit Romans 7:4 and you'll see what I mean.

> Therefore, my brethren, *you also have become dead to the law* through the body of Christ, that you may be married to another—to Him who was raised from the dead, *that we should bear fruit to God.* (emphasis added)

Please note that final phrase. Do you want to be a fruit-bearing Christian? Then make sure you are connected to the right husband. In John 15:5, Jesus told His disciples:

> I am the vine, you are the branches. He who abides in Me, and I in him, bears much fruit; for without Me you can do nothing.

The only way you're going to bear fruit is to be connected (married) to Jesus. He is a husband that can cause you to be fruitful. He's not impotent. In contrast, the Law is a sterile, loveless husband who cannot make you fruitful. And there is yet a third limitation to your old husband.

Number Three: The Law can't make you righteous. That's the message of Galatians 2:21: "I do not set aside the grace of God; for if righteousness comes through the law, then Christ died in vain." This is why Paul devotes so much time in Romans to explaining that Abraham's righteousness was "imputed" to him by God because of his faith, not his good behavior.

Remember, the Father's goal from the very beginning was to restore us to Himself. The unrighteousness that attached itself to mankind in the Fall opened up a huge chasm between us and Him. Our separation problem was really a righteousness problem. And as Paul points out to the Galatians in the verse above, there was no reason for Jesus to come and die if the Law had the power to produce righteousness in us. Paul also declares that wrongly expecting Law keeping to produce righteousness is, in effect, setting aside the grace of God.

Again, if righteousness could possibly come through the Law, why would Jesus die on the cross? It can come to us only as a grace-gift made available in Jesus (see Romans 5:17). In fact, in the new birth, we are gifted with Jesus' own righteousness. And Jesus' righteousness is the gold standard of righteousness. (More on this in the next chapter!)

I suspect you're beginning to see what a terrible husband the Law was. And what an upgrade you and I received when we were released from that first marriage by "dying" with Christ and being reborn into marriage with Him instead.

It is far better to be married to a wonderful *person* than it is to an impossible list. So much better! And yet...

Many times we find ourselves behaving as if we're still married to

It is far better to be married to a wonderful *person* than it is to an impossible list.

the Law. We often think, believe, and behave as if we were still obligated to love, honor, and obey that list of rules and regulations. But as the passage with which we began this study pointed out, marriage vows are only "till death do us part," and you and I have died in Christ.

I know a number of people who have a previous marriage in their background. Well, here is an illuminating thought experiment.

What would you think of a woman who had previously been married to a hard, harsh, relentlessly critical perfectionist, but is now married to the kindest, gentlest, most supportive man you could possibly imagine? Now imagine that she consistently tries to impress husband number two by doing all the things that husband number one demanded. Imagine she goes out of her way to avoid doing the things that bugged husband number one, dresses as he preferred that she dress, and generally puts herself through a lot of grief and toil doing the things that pleased her ex. Even worse, imagine that she told her current husband, "Honey, I've got some news that I know is going to bless you. I've been going over to my first husband's house to serve him and do things for him because I think that will make our marriage better."

You'd think she was out of her mind. You'd think she was foolish.

Nevertheless, countless Christians do essentially the same thing. Multitudes are trying to impress their new and better husband, Jesus, by keeping a good relationship with their first husband, the

> Multitudes are trying to impress their new and better husband, Jesus, by keeping a good relationship with their first husband, the Law.

Law. Try that literally and see how it works out for you. No wonder Paul practically shouted on paper, "Foolish Galatians, who has bewitched you…!"

The gospel is, literally, good news. Here's good news for you and me. We don't serve a list; we love a Person.

Now as the implications of this chapter sink in, I suspect some questions have arisen in your mind. Questions like, "The Law said, 'Don't murder.' Is it okay to murder now that I know I'm no longer married to the Law?" That, and many other reasonable questions you are likely to have, you will find answers to in the chapters ahead. So let's keep going!

CHAPTER 11

BY GRACE: BETTER RIGHTEOUSNESS

We're on a hillside in Galilee roughly two thousand years ago and minds are being blown. A crowd of Jesus followers has gathered to hear the wonder-working Rabbi that has all of Israel buzzing with excitement explain this coming kingdom that has been the theme of His preaching all over Judea and Galilee.

Jesus and His core followers have been bouncing from north to south and back again visiting every village and synagogue in the land. How do we know that? Matthew 9:35 says so: "Then Jesus went about *all the cities and villages, teaching in their synagogues,* preaching the gospel of the kingdom, and healing every sickness and every disease among the people."

And in each place, He has seemingly echoed the talking points of His cousin, John the Baptizer. Those points spoke of two things. A coming judgment upon Israel that called for repentance. And the imminent arrival of the "kingdom of God" or the "kingdom of heaven." (Please note: Matthew's Gospel consistently substitutes the phrase *kingdom of heaven* for *kingdom of God* so as to avoid offending the Jewish readers who are his primary target audience. Matthew's Gospel seems especially focused on persuading Jewish people that Jesus is the promised Messiah of Israel.)

John's preaching could be summed up with a single line: "Repent, for the kingdom of heaven is at hand!" (Matthew 3:2). But his pronouncements also included:

- Warnings of coming "wrath" (Matthew 3:7).
- Imagery of an ax that was already poised at the base of many of the trees of Israel, which would soon be cut down and thrown into the fire (see Matthew 3:10).
- And imagery of One who would come after Him carrying a winnowing fork, to separate Israel's chaff from her wheat. The wheat would be gathered into a barn whereas the chaff would experience "unquenchable fire" (Matthew 3:12).

We saw in a previous chapter that in A.D. 70, forty years after Jesus' death and resurrection, Roman armies destroyed Jerusalem. In their march through Israel, hundreds of thousands were killed, and many of the remainder sold in the Roman slave markets. John's prophetic preaching warned of this very event. But if you've read the Gospels, you know that the One whom John said would follow his own "forerunner" ministry was Jesus. And so, we find this:

> *Now after John was put in prison*, Jesus came to Galilee, preaching the gospel of the kingdom of God, and saying, "The time is fulfilled, and the kingdom of God is at hand. Repent, and believe in the gospel." (Mark 1:14–15, emphasis added)

Do you see it? As soon as the prophet John was thrown in prison, Jesus took up his cousin's prophetic mantle and message, with two significant additions to John's "Repent, for the kingdom of God is at hand" message. First, Jesus declared that, now that His public ministry had begun, "the time is fulfilled." Second, He positioned the warning about the need for repentance as "the gospel"—in other words, *good news*. Prophetic warnings about impending destruction are not usually considered good news, but as events will show, this one was. It would be good news for those in Israel who believed and received His message. Indeed, it would be good news for the whole world. Good news because the new was much better than the old in every conceivable way.

> Prophetic warnings about impending destruction are not usually considered good news, but as events will show, this one was.

Throughout Jesus' prophetic preaching ministry, He, like John, would warn of a coming winnowing process in which wheat would be separated from chaff in Israel. In fact, many of Jesus' parables about the coming kingdom were sorting and separating metaphors like that one. He would speak of wheat being separated from tares. (The tares, or weeds, burned up.) Sheep being separated from goats. And nets full of fish being sorted—some being kept and others being tossed away. Two kinds of bridesmaids—one group that would make it to the wedding and another that wouldn't. Two kinds of royal wedding guests—friends of the king who refused the invitation, and strangers rounded up from the highways and byways.

Yes, symbolically embedded in Jesus' preaching about the kingdom in all the synagogues and villages is the message that some hearers would be chaff, tares, goats, bad fish, and bridesmaids that missed out. Others would be wheat, sheep, good fish, and brides-maids that made it to the party.

Another group of parables carried another surprising message about this kingdom Jesus said was "at hand," "near," and "upon you." At that time, the universal Jewish assumption about the kingdom was that it involved a physical, sudden, and complete restoration of David's glorious throne in Jerusalem, with David's descendant, the Messiah, sitting upon it. But many of Jesus' parables about the kingdom suggest something very different.

Repeatedly, when asked about it, Jesus would begin a parable with the words, "The kingdom of God is like…" Among the things it was like were:

- A tiny mustard seed that, over time, grows into a massive tree (see Matthew 13:31–32).
- A tiny pinch of yeast that slowly, progressively leavens the entire loaf (see Matthew 13:33).

These similes suggest the opposite of something sudden and instantly mature. Instead, they suggest the kingdom would be something that would start small and progressively grow over a long period of time. All of this is the prelude to, and the context of, this hillside gathering in Galilee we have just joined.

Everywhere He went Jesus had preached the gospel of the kingdom, but He had done so in ways that completely bewildered and confounded

> Everywhere He went Jesus had preached the gospel of the kingdom, but He had done so in ways that completely bewildered and confounded all the prevailing assumptions.

all the prevailing assumptions. Today's sermon will be no different. We and the other listeners are about to hear what will one day be called the Sermon on the Mount. Among the hearers are Pharisees, scribes, and other devout Jews who actually think they are successfully keeping the Law in every aspect. Later on, Jesus will have an encounter with another such person, a "rich young ruler," who will ask Jesus what he is required to do to obtain eternal life (Matthew 19:16). Jesus, knowing that perfect righteousness was necessary to bridge the sin-gap and stand before God, said, "Keep the commandments [perfectly and fully]" (v. 17). Do you recall what this young man's astonishing answer was?

The young man said to Him, "All these I have kept from my youth. What do I still lack?" (v. 20)

Let that sink in. Devout Jews at that time had carefully parsed and organized the Torah and found 613 commandments to follow. At the core of these were those Ten Commandments God gave Moses. And this person was confident that he had obeyed *all* of them all of his life. *Box, checked! What else ya got?*

Now, Jesus once said the greatest of those 613 commandments was to love God with all your heart, soul, mind, and strength (see Mark 12:30). So He gave the self-confident young man an instruction that would put his claim to the test. Jesus said, "Go, sell what you have and give to the poor, and you will have treasure in heaven; and come, follow Me" (Matthew 19:21). Was love for God really the highest love in this man's life? Was he truly in obedience to this, the greatest of all commandments? Or was there something he loved more than God? You know the answer to that question. With a single instruction, Jesus exposed the man's claim to perfect righteousness as a lie. (Which, by the way, is a violation of another commandment, the one against bearing false witness.)

Here in the crowd at the Sermon on the Mount, Jesus has a lot of people, young and old, just like that rich, young ruler. They, too, believe they are keeping all the commandments. They believe they have a form of righteousness. Indeed, they do. It's just not an adequate form. It's not true righteousness—the kind that allows a human being to have a personal friendship with the holy God of the universe. Pointing that out will be a big focus of Jesus' sermon today.

For example, for those in the crowd who think they've obeyed the Sixth Commandment—"You shall not murder"—Jesus will tell them that being angry at their brother, or even just calling him an idiot, is a violation (see Matthew 5:22). For those pleased and proud that they have never committed adultery, prohibited in the Seventh Commandment, Jesus has bad news as well. Even looking on a woman with lustful thoughts is a violation (see v. 28). Jesus will tell those who have justified a divorce on flimsy grounds that they are out of bounds as well (see v. 32). He will also tell them that the kind of righteousness that makes one fit for the kingdom of God looks like loving your enemies; turning the other cheek when you're slapped; cheerfully going the extra mile; and, when asked for your coat, giving it gladly and throwing in your shirt as a bonus. All of which will sound utterly impossible to His hearers on this day (because it is). And that was the point.

Piece by piece, Jesus will dismantle their smug, self-satisfied belief in their Old Covenant righteousness until there is nothing but a pile of smoldering rubble. Why? Because they desperately needed a Savior but didn't think they did. They didn't know they

utterly lacked the kind of righteousness that could reconnect them to
intimate relationship with God.

> Piece by piece,
> Jesus will dismantle
> their smug, self-
> satisfied belief in
> their Old Covenant
> righteousness until
> there is nothing but
> a pile of smoldering
> rubble.

Jesus came to give the gift of that
kind of righteousness, but people
who think they're already righteous
will never receive His gift.

Which is why Jesus opens the
Sermon on the Mount with a series
of "Blessed are..." or "Happy are..."
statements. We call this series of statements the Beatitudes. This list
describes the kind of people among his Jewish listeners who will have
a heart soft enough to receive and enter this new, coming kingdom
that He's been preaching about all over the country. All of His sorting and separating parables make it clear that some will have a heart
to receive this good news, but many won't. What kind of people *will*
receive it? According to his list:

the poor in spirit (v. 3)
those who mourn (v. 4)
the meek (v. 5)
the merciful (v. 7)
the pure in heart (v. 8)
the peacemakers (v. 9)
those persecuted for righteousness' sake (v. 10)

All of these should be happy because they have the kinds of
hearts that will be receptive to the proclamation of the New Covenant kingdom when it arrives, and in it will experience the meeting

of their deepest needs. But in the middle of that list, Jesus will say this:

> Blessed are those who hunger and thirst for *righteousness*, for they shall be filled. (Matthew 5:6, emphasis added)

Of course, people who already think they are righteous don't hunger and thirst for it. People like that rich young ruler. People like the scribes and the Pharisees. So just a few sentences later Jesus drops this bomb.

> For I say to you, that unless your righteousness *exceeds the righteousness of the scribes and Pharisees*, you will by no means enter the kingdom of heaven. (Matthew 5:20, emphasis added)

What a stunner this is for Jesus' listeners. In this culture, the Pharisees and scribes are considered the gold standard for righteousness. Yet here Jesus declares that only those who have an even *better* form of righteousness—true righteousness, which means being perfectly right with God—can enter the coming kingdom. This would not have sounded like good news to any person in the crowd. On the contrary, this would have been cause for despair for His hearers. But that was precisely the point. As Isaiah 64:6 declares, "All our righteousnesses are like filthy rags." The same is true for you and me.

On the most awesome good-behavior and good-works day you've ever had in your life, that homemade righteousness you cooked up was filthy rags in comparison with the righteousness needed to partner with God as a friend in this life, and in eternity.

Imagine you're standing on the sidewalk beside the Empire State Building. The level of righteousness necessary to be restored to what Adam and Eve forfeited is at the very top of that mooring mast at the peak of the building, 1,454 feet above street level. Now imagine the ugliest, most sin-filled, most selfish, most fleshly day you've ever had. That day puts a mark on the building half an inch above the sidewalk. Now bring out your best day of holy living. A day in which you did a lot of the "dos" and avoided almost all of the "don'ts." A day in which you managed to get up early and check the "quiet time" box. Didn't snap at family members. Smiled at strangers. Gave panhandlers spare change. Petted dogs. Didn't glare at the guy who cut you off in traffic. Didn't lie (much). Didn't covet other people's stuff (much). And certainly didn't cheat, steal, or murder. How high up the skyscraper would that day get you? It would put a mark one inch high. Or about half an inch higher than your worst day.

This is the point of Jesus' sermon. This is why Jesus tells His audience (and us) that they need a type of righteousness exceeding that of the scribes and Pharisees.

What Jesus' audience can't possibly know or understand in this moment is that His perfect life and sacrificial death are going to make it possible to receive, by faith, *His* righteousness as a grace-gift!

Keep in mind what we learned in the previous chapters. The core purpose of the Law was to make us aware of our sinfulness and our need for a Savior. The Sermon on the Mount had this same purpose.

> The core purpose of the Law was to make us aware of our sinfulness and our need for a Savior. The Sermon on the Mount had this same purpose.

The blood of animal sacrifices in the Old Covenant system could "cover" sin for a year. But...

> But in those sacrifices there is a reminder of sins every year. For it is not possible that the blood of bulls and goats could take away sins. (Hebrews 10:3–4)

But the shedding of Jesus' sinless blood carried the power to wash sin and its guilt away completely.

Again, *righteousness* means "in right standing with God." Here's what we have to understand, though. In the kingdom, that is, in this new and better covenant, I am not in right standing with God because I do right things. I can't ever possibly do enough right things to become right with God. Trying hard to do enough right things only gets me the false, prideful faux-righteousness of the scribes and Pharisees. It's a righteousness rooted in comparison with other people, rather than one compared to the pristine holiness of God. That's a righteousness that Jesus declared inadequate. Besides, as James 2:10 reveals, "For whoever shall keep the whole law, and yet stumble in one *point*, he is guilty of all."

No, I am in right standing with God because Jesus did everything right, and by faith I am in Him. I have received, as a grace gift, *His* righteousness. In fact, the miracle of the new birth wraps you, or clothes you, in Jesus' perfect righteousness. The prophet Isaiah foresaw this:

> I will greatly rejoice in the LORD, My soul shall be joyful in my God; For He has clothed me with the garments of salvation, He has covered me with the robe of righteousness... (Isaiah 61:10a)

Paul describes this miracle here:

For as many of you as were baptized into Christ *have put on Christ.* (Galatians 3:27, emphasis added)

And here:

For He made Him who knew no sin to be sin for us, that we might become the righteousness of God in Him. (2 Corinthians 5:21)

What an upgrade this is! We receive, as an unmerited, unearned, undeserved gift, the flawless righteousness of Jesus. No wonder this creates right standing with God. Is Jesus welcome in God's presence? Yes! Is the Father delighted to see His only begotten Son? Of course! And salvation submerges us...clothes us...wraps us...in Jesus. Read the first chapter of Ephesians and note all the appearances of the phrases "in Him," "in Christ," "in the Beloved." This means blood-washed believers are as welcome in God's presence as Jesus is. It means the Father is delighted to see you, too. It means it is as appropriate for us to be with God, to know God, to partner with God in carrying out His plans and purposes on earth, as Jesus. Why? Because we're *in Him* and have received His righteousness.

> We receive, as an unmerited, unearned, undeserved gift, the flawless righteousness of Jesus.

Again, this righteousness is a gift. But it gets even better. Because of my right standing with God, my desires begin to change as I hang around Him. Beholding the presence of God begins to transform me from the inside out. I increasingly have a desire to do right things. My growth in God becomes a process in which my behavior progressively comes into alignment with who I already am in God's eyes! God first imparts Jesus' righteousness to us, then sets Himself to the process of transforming us into His image (see Romans 8:29).

My behavior and actions aren't irrelevant. But I'm not righteous because I do good things. More and more, I do good things because I've been declared righteous. Yet so many believers have the cart before the horse. We're not saved *by* good works. We're saved *to* good works. That's the clear message of Ephesians 2:8–10. You'll recall that we began this entire study with the first two of these three verses. Now note the verse that immediately follows:

> We're not saved *by* good works. We're saved *to* good works.

For by grace you have been saved through faith, and that not of yourselves; it is the gift of God, not of works, lest anyone should boast. *For we are His workmanship, created in Christ Jesus for good works, which God prepared beforehand that we should walk in them.* (emphasis added)

Without a doubt, God does want us to live righteously—to exhibit righteous behavior. But this is impossible outside of a living, breathing connection to God by His Spirit. We don't behave well in order to earn our connection to God. Our connection to God transforms our desires and, ultimately, our behavior. And we have the opportunity to have that connection to God because He has both imputed and imparted Jesus' own righteousness to us!

Too many believers let shame and guilt keep them out of God's presence. This is because they have forgotten, or have never been taught, that they never come to God in their own flawed righteousness. They can't! They always and only come in Jesus' righteousness. The tragedy is that it is only in God's presence—in intimate fellowship, conversation, and communion with Him—that they can experience the transformation that changes those very behaviors that cause their shame and guilt. When I've acted unrighteously, when I've sinned, when I've made a mess of things, that's when I must run to my Father. There the light of His presence will illuminate the dark, unrenewed corners of my soul so they can be made new. Only that light can expose the lies I've believed that are the root of my patterns of sin and failure. Only there, at the throne of grace, will I find mercy and help in my time of need (see Hebrews 4:16). But if I don't understand the reality that I have received a better righteousness because I am in Christ, I will let my shame keep me away from the only place that can fix what's broken.

No wonder they call the truth about who Jesus is and what He accomplished "good news." One glorious facet of that good news is that, by grace, we have received an extraordinary gift—Jesus' righteousness. His right standing with the Father. A righteousness infinitely better than anything we could ever produce on our own.

But that's not the only "better" aspect of what Jesus made possible in His new and better covenant. We have more to explore.

CHAPTER 12

BY GRACE: BETTER REST

Let's call her Martha. Martha loves Jesus with all her heart. She has since she was a child. But Martha is exhausted. Physically, emotionally, and spiritually exhausted. For her entire life as a Christian, she's been a little like a duck. Seemingly calm and serene above the surface but unseen, just below the surface, paddling furiously. Now after decades of striving and struggling, she is contemplating giving up.

She has always wanted, with everything in her, to please her heavenly Father. She still does, but recently she has begun to despair of ever attaining that goal. You see, as a child in Sunday school, Martha absorbed several lessons deeply. She learned that a person carrying unconfessed sin cannot stand in the presence of an infinitely holy God. A sinful person approaching God would be instantly consumed by the fire of His pure glory. She learned that when she got saved, all her past sins were washed away by the blood of Jesus. She was also taught that that same blood was available to wash away any sins she committed *after* salvation, as long as she repented and confessed them.

She has always known she is supposed to be avoiding all the "don'ts." And from her childhood forward she has done a pretty good job of abstaining from biggies like murdering, robbing banks, and committing adultery. But she knows that there are no little sins. She has been taught, correctly, that sins of the heart and mind are equally offensive in God's eyes. Sins like envy, jealousy, coveting, little white lies, and outbursts of anger. And throughout her life, she's found these "don'ts" far harder to avoid. So she was taught to carefully examine herself before approaching God in prayer. This was necessary, she was told, because every sin created a separation between her and God. She unquestioningly believes that her access to God's throne room and presence is blocked until she pauses to deal with recent sins.

As a girl in school, her thoughts would turn to God frequently throughout the day. The trials, trouble, and traumas that accompany life in junior high and high school frequently made her want to turn to God in prayer for help and comfort, but that impulse was always instantly followed by an arresting, fearful thought: *But my sins...*

But this isn't the only thing fueling the fire of Martha's burnout. As she grew up in church, she learned of an additional class of sins. Sins of omission, they're called. Not only was she obligated to avoid all the "don'ts," there were many "dos" she was supposed to be doing. Countless boxes that needed to be checked if God was truly going to be pleased with her. Frequent church attendance, a daily quiet time, and sharing her faith topped a long list of things she ought to be doing.

As she grew older, she heard others speaking of having a deep, satisfying, intimate relationship with a God they knew as a loving Father. Oh, how she longed for that. But she assumed that these people lived more holy lives than she did. *They must sin a lot less than I do*, she thought. She unconsciously assumed they had earned or qualified for this level of intimacy through good behavior and good works. So her desire for more intimacy with God fueled countless resolutions to do *better*. To *try harder*. (A friend of mine says that the entire teaching of the Church concerning spiritual growth can be summed up in two words: *Try harder*.)

Martha has rarely doubted that she will go to heaven when she dies. But she has constantly doubted that God is pleased with her. She has never had any assurance that the little girl inside her was accepted and received and welcome in God's lap. Others might have that assurance. But not her. The tattered Bible she's had since high school now just falls open to Psalm 51, David's prayer of heartbroken repentance after committing adultery and murder. She knows it by heart:

> Have mercy upon me, O God, According to Your
> lovingkindness;
> According to the multitude of Your tender mercies, Blot out
> my transgressions.
> Wash me thoroughly from my iniquity, And cleanse me from
> my sin.
> For I acknowledge my transgressions, And my sin is always
> before me.
> Against You, You only, have I sinned, And done this evil in
> Your sight—
> That You may be found just when You speak, And blameless
> when You judge. (Psalm 51:1–4)

Each time Martha visits this chapter in an endeavor to feel clean enough and acceptable enough to approach God in prayer, verse eleven sends an icy shock of fear through her soul: "Do not cast me away from Your presence, And do not take Your Holy Spirit from me," David wrote. Fully aware that God knows her innermost thoughts, Martha has lived her entire life in the dread that God might one day get weary of her continual need for forgiveness and do what David pleaded with God *not* to do. That is, lock her out of His throne room once and for all.

Is it any wonder she is exhausted? Should we marvel that she is teetering on the edge of despair? If only she could be like her good friend, we'll call her Mary, who is one of those people who obviously enjoys a close, intimate, life-giving relationship with God.

Mary, too, was raised in a Christian home, but at some point along the way, she encountered some teaching that brought her the concepts you've encountered in the previous chapters. She learned that through the new birth, she died to obligation to the Law and that instead she was wedded to Jesus. And that Jesus became her complete fulfillment of all the Law required. She discovered that she never again had to approach God on the basis of *her* righteousness but that, by grace, she had literally "become" the righteousness of Jesus Christ.

All of this meant that she viewed the door to God's presence as always wide open. Once she renewed her mind to those truths— once she rooted her identity in them—she began to feel free to fly to His arms of love at any moment of need or crisis.

What's more, she no longer viewed spending time with God as a box to be checked in order to qualify for blessing or answered prayer. Fellowshipping with her Creator became a privilege, not a prerequisite. An opportunity not an ought. That meant her times with the Father became a source of joy in her life. With Him she received strength and nourishment and instruction. What's more,

Fellowshipping with her Creator became a privilege, not a prerequisite. An opportunity not an ought.

in His presence she experienced transformation. Her desires began to change. Where her friend Martha had spent her entire life trying (and failing) to change from the outside in through raw self-discipline and willpower, Mary was experiencing seemingly effortless change from the inside out.

Mary had been taught to live in God without the fear of rejection. Without the fear of judgment. Without the fear of not qualifying for what Jesus died to provide. In contrast, Martha's well-meaning teachers and mentors were afraid for her to ever stop being afraid. Terrified that if she ever realized that her relationship with God didn't hinge on her good behavior, she'd just go wild and turn God's gift of grace into a license to sin. Ironically, the graceless legalism that she had absorbed early in life was actually stirring up her flesh and desire to do wrong. Martha was trapped in the nightmare Paul describes in Romans 7:15: "I don't really understand myself, for I want to do what is right, but I don't do it. Instead, I do what I hate" (NLT). This, in turn, keeps Martha under a constant, crushing weight of condemnation. We saw in a previous chapter that the Law has a ministry of condemnation. And our poor Martha is a recipient of that "ministry" every day.

How different are the lives of these two Jesus-loving daughters of God? One is living in bondage to rules. Another is being led by the Spirit. Think about that in the light of the words from Romans Chapter 8:

For as many as are led by the Spirit of God, these are sons of God. For you did not receive *the spirit of bondage again to fear,* but you received the Spirit of adoption by whom we cry out, "Abba, Father." (v. 14–15, emphasis added)

There is another biblical model for understanding the difference between these two believers' lives in God. That model is found in the third and fourth chapters of Hebrews and can be called Striving Versus Rest.

We've already noted that the book of Hebrews was initially written to Jewish believers and to Jews considering faith in Jesus. In these key chapters, the writer compares the ancient generation of Israelites who, through fearful unbelief, forfeited their opportunity to go into the Promised Land, to people in his day who, through unbelief, were refusing to go into the new Promised Land of the New Covenant. Repeatedly, the author describes the original Promised Land as a place of "rest" (see Hebrews 3:11). Then in the opening verses of Chapter 4 we read this about God's invitation to enter into rest in the New Covenant:

Therefore, since a promise remains of entering His rest, let us fear lest any of you seem to have come short of it... *For we who have believed do enter that rest*... (v. 1, 3a, emphasis added)

And in verse 11:

Let us therefore *be diligent to enter that rest*, lest anyone fall according to the same example of disobedience. (emphasis added)

We're exhorted to "be diligent" to enter into the rest that God has provided in Jesus. But how? What does it mean to enter that kind of rest? The two verses preceding verse eleven answer that question.

> There remains, then, a Sabbath-rest for the people of God; *for anyone who enters God's rest also rests from their works*, just as God did from his. (Hebrews 4:9–10 NIV, emphasis added)

There you have it. Fully entering into the finished work of Jesus on the cross represents a type of Sabbath rest from our works. And in the event we're unsure about what that means, the writer spells it out for us. God spent six days in active work in crafting Creation. Then, on the seventh, He entered an extended, ongoing rest—His Sabbath. God had commanded the Israelites to remember and honor that by instituting a seventh-day rest in Israel.

The passage above says that we can and must enter God's rest by resting from our works, just as God did from His. The larger context of Hebrews makes it clear that resting from your works doesn't mean quitting your job and lying around on the couch all day. Note that a few chapters later, this same writer exhorts us to "let us lay aside every weight, and the sin which so easily ensnares us, and *let us run with endurance* the race that is set before us" (Hebrews 12:1, emphasis added).

No, to enter God's Sabbath rest means to stop working, striving, and struggling to *earn* or *deserve* your relational standing with God, and instead receive the grace-gift of what Jesus earned and deserved on your behalf. It means an end to striving to *qualify* for intimate relationship with God through Law keeping and rule following, and instead allow Jesus to be your qualification. Remember, grace is unmerited, unearned, and undeserved.

Entering into God's Sabbath rest means an end to the exhausting, discouraging, shame-filled cycle of struggle and defeat that is the only possible result of living Martha's "try harder" brand of Christianity. It means stepping into the Promised Land of living in Jesus' righteousness and qualification, just as Mary did. There, in your wide-open access to God, you are transformed and changed "from glory to glory":

> But we all, with unveiled face, beholding as in a mirror the glory of the Lord, are being transformed into the same image from glory to glory, just as by the Spirit of the Lord. (2 Corinthians 3:18)

Now let's pull together the Promised Land and Sabbath imagery of Hebrews Chapters 3 and 4, and apply it directly to you.

Imagine that you've been wandering around in a hot, dry, scrubby, rocky desert for what seems like an eternity. This wilderness has been a terrible place to try to live. A harsh, inhospitable wasteland filled with struggle and hardship. You've needed miracles of provision just to survive in this place. Then one day you arrive at a river.

You discover that God has led you to the border of an amazing land, just as He'd promised He would. You look across and can hardly believe your eyes. It's green, not brown and beige. Lakes, rivers, and streams are seemingly everywhere. Regular, seasonal rains water its bountiful fields, vineyards, and orchards. The place just seems to be bursting with abundance. You know that living in a place like that would be beyond a dream.

Amazingly, God has said, "This land is yours. I'm giving it to you. I've even gone before you to make it possible for you to possess it" (see Deuteronomy 1:8 and 31:8). Now only one question remains. Will you believe what you've just been told? If so, you'll confidently head across that river into this new place where your striving and struggling and scraping and scrounging come to an end.

The same question stands before every born-again believer. God's Word declares, "There remains, then, a Sabbath-rest for the people of God." Will you believe what you've been told?

> Your salvation was, figuratively, your deliverance from slavery in Egypt.

Your salvation was, figuratively, your deliverance from slavery in Egypt. With a mighty hand, God delivered you out of the bondage of sin through the sacrifice of a Passover Lamb.

Now, in His kindness, He has led you to the edge of a good land, flowing with milk and honey. A place of rest. Sabbath rest... in which you lay down a pride-driven need to earn and deserve. Yet the choice remains with you. It's a faith-choice.

So we see that because of their unbelief they were not able to enter his rest. God's promise of entering his rest still stands... (Hebrews 3:19, 4:1a NLT)

The Marys among us have crossed over. A *better* rest still awaits the Marthas. And they are many. I can hear them asking now, "But what about good works? Don't my works matter?" It's an important question. The answer lies just ahead.

CHAPTER 13

BY GRACE: BETTER WORKS

I won't keep you in suspense. Yes! That's the answer to the question I asked at the end of the previous chapter.

Yes. Of course, your actions—your works, good and bad—matter. Stepping into the grace and rest of the New Covenant doesn't make your actions and choices irrelevant. The Bible is clear that there are rewards in heaven. (We'll talk more about those before we close this chapter.) And in this life, sin invariably produces bad outcomes. Perhaps you've noticed that everything the Bible calls sin tends to either be self-destructive, others-destructive, or society-destructive—and often all three. God's moral Law reflects His infinite love for people, so it's no wonder God declares these things off limits. They hurt the objects of God's love. The more you do of what God labels sin, the worse your life gets. So of course your behavior matters.

Your works matter. It's just that there are two kinds of works. And by now you won't be surprised to learn that because of the amazing grace of our God, one of those kinds of works is far better than the other.

You met Martha and her friend Mary in the previous chapter. As a casual observer looking on from the outside, you'd likely say the two women appear to be living very similar Christian lives.

Both volunteer and serve at their church. Both faithfully tithe. Both give offerings to support missions. Both help the poor. Both witness—telling others they encounter that God loves them and Jesus is their only hope for salvation. Yet one woman is exhausted and miserable, and frequently feels far from God. The other, despite rough days from time to time, is generally at peace, is filled with joy, and enjoys near-constant communion with her heavenly Father. What's going on here? The disparity lies in the difference between "good works" and "dead works." Let me explain.

First, I need to be clear that God is very *pro* good works. He's a fan. Which is why Jesus said: "Let your light so shine before men, that they may see *your good works* and glorify your Father in heaven" (Matthew 5:16, emphasis added). And I have pointed out previously that the verse immediately following our key passage—Ephesians 2:8–9—declares that although we are not saved *by* good works, we are saved *for* good works:

> For we are His workmanship, *created in Christ Jesus for good works*, which God prepared beforehand that we should walk in them. (Ephesians 2:10, emphasis added)

You were created in your mother's womb the first time. But you were re-created—born again—when you surrendered your life to Jesus and were baptized into Him. In fact, according to this verse, the good works you can do "in Christ Jesus" were prepared and planned before you were even saved. As 2 Corinthians 5:17 says: "Therefore, if anyone is in Christ, he is a new creation." Please understand, this new creation—*you*—was designed by the Designer for good works! Cars are designed to run on roads. Planes are designed to fly. New-creation humans are designed to do good stuff.

> Cars are designed to run on roads. Planes are designed to fly. New-creation humans are designed to do good stuff.

With that in mind, brace yourself for another Robert Morris profound saying. You might want to highlight this...

"Good works are good."

No, it's true. It's good to do good works. There is a reason we call them *good* works. It's right there in the name! But there is another kind of works mentioned in the Bible. Dead works. Would you be shocked to learn that *dead* works aren't nearly as good as *good* works?

Learning about them will require jumping back into the book of Hebrews. Keep in mind, this neglected book is probably the New Testament's clearest, most thorough explanation of the New Covenant that Jesus established through His sacrificial death. It's the covenant you and I are in if we're saved, so it's helpful to know about it. In the previous chapter we spent some time in Hebrews Chapters 3 and 4. Well in Chapter 5, the Holy Spirit–inspired writer expresses some frustration with the recipients of his letter. He says:

> About this subject [Jesus and His ministry as our High Priest] there is much for us to say, and it is hard to explain since you have become sluggish in hearing. For although you ought to be teachers by this time, again you need someone to teach you the basics of God's sayings. You have come to need milk, not solid food. (Hebrews 5:11–12 TLV, addition mine)

Let me paraphrase. So basically, he's calling his target readers big babies. He says they have been Christians long enough to have grown up into the meat-eating stage of maturity—in fact, they should be teaching others by now—yet they were still needing milk. This prompts the writer of Hebrews, just a few verses later, to urge his readers to grow up!

> Therefore, leaving the discussion of the elementary principles of Christ, let us go on to perfection [maturity]...(Hebrews 6:1a, addition mine)

What are these elementary principles of the faith from which these believers should have already graduated? We don't have to guess. The writer immediately lists them:

> ...not laying again the foundation of *repentance from dead works* and of faith toward God, of the doctrine of baptisms, of laying on of hands, of resurrection of the dead, and of eternal judgment. (Hebrews 6:1b–2, emphasis added)

At the top of this list of six things these people should have long since learned in Jesus Kindergarten was "repentance from dead works."

But what does that mean? What are these dead works that they should have long ago repented of? As is so often the case with interpreting Scripture, context is the key. Keep in mind, the book of Hebrews is written first and foremost to born-again Jewish people. They had come out of a deep, ancient tradition, which taught that Law keeping and doing good works made you acceptable to God. But as much of the book of Hebrews, as well as large sections of the

Apostle Paul's writings make clear, our futile attempts at Law keeping could produce nothing but death. So one of the first things new Jewish believers needed to understand is the very thing we revisited early in this chapter. Namely that we're saved *for* good works, not *by* good works.

Trying to get or keep a relationship with God through works makes those works "dead." They have no life in them. Take a look at how *The Message* paraphrase handles that verse about elementary principles and repentance from dead works:

> So come on, let's leave the preschool fingerpainting exercises on Christ and get on with the grand work of art. Grow up in Christ. The basic foundational truths are in place: turning your back on "salvation by self-help" and turning in trust toward God... (Hebrews 6:1)

"Salvation by self-help" is a good way to phrase what the Bible is describing here. So dead works are anything good you do in an effort to *earn* acceptance from God. (You can't earn what Jesus purchased for you and offers as a free gift.) Dead works are like the citizens of Babel who decided they were going to build a tower to heaven and thereby make a name for themselves (see Genesis 11:4).

In contrast, good works are all the things you do as a natural outgrowth of your life-connection and fellowship with God. *Connection* is the operative word there. You probably know that in John 15:5 Jesus compares himself to a vine:

> I am the vine, you are the branches. He who abides in Me, and I in him, bears much fruit; for without Me you can do nothing.

Note that word *abides*. We'll be seeing it again in a bit. Jesus is revealing that any real and lasting fruit we bear comes from our connection to Him, that is, from being in Him and Him in us. Yet so many of us struggle to accept His statement that apart from Him we "can do nothing."

> The original recipients of the letter to the Hebrews were still in Jesus Kindergarten because they needed to repent of trying to earn their connection to God.

The original recipients of the letter to the Hebrews were still in Jesus Kindergarten because they needed to repent of trying to earn their connection to God. Again, you can't earn what can only be received as a gift. Apart from connection to Him, you can bear no fruit. But as Jesus suggests here, good works do result quite naturally from being in connection to Him. Your life-giving connection of rest as a beloved son or daughter of God can't help but result in a lifestyle of good works.

There is a reason the title of this book is titled *Grace, Period.*, rather than *Grace Plus*, or *Grace And*, or *Grace But*. "Sabbath rest" means putting your full weight upon what Jesus accomplished on the cross—with nothing added. It means not insulting God's grace through prideful efforts to earn your seat at God's sumptuous banqueting table. It's a pattern of living that doesn't insult the enormous price God paid—His only begotten Son—to purchase for you the most extravagant gift ever given.

There is a reason God put Abraham to sleep when establishing a covenant with him. In a parity covenant ceremony, ordinarily the two parties making the covenant walk between the pieces of sacrificed animals. But read the account in Genesis Chapter 15: You'll see that Abraham tries to "help" by frantically running around scaring off vultures that are trying to land on the carcasses. So God puts Abraham into a deep sleep (rest). In a dream, Abraham then sees a smoking torch and a burning oven—which symbolize the Father and the Son—pass between the carcasses instead.

Let's just pause here for a moment to savor the extraordinary beauty and symmetry of God's plan of redemption. In the details of this covenant ceremony with Abraham, God is foreshadowing the parity covenant He will one day establish with His only begotten Son for our benefit. In a sense, Abraham represents us. As a fallen human, he cannot enter into a parity covenant with God Most High. But by entering into the grace of rest, he gets to participate in it because he has a divine proxy in the ceremony.

It all supports this one, vital, central truth about grace. Our activity and actions in God should be *from*, not *for*. Here's what I mean.

We do good works *from* our relationship with God, not *for* our relationship with God. So many precious sons and daughters of God are wearing themselves out striving, in their own strength, in the hope of purchasing—through good behavior and good works—enough credits with God to get a prayer answered. In this mindset, a loving heavenly Father becomes a sort of heavenly vending machine. Insert enough good-works tokens and you get to pull a lever to get a prize or a treat. How destructive this transactional approach is to the intimate, Father-child relationship God went to such extremes to make possible for us. But please understand, this doesn't at all mean the grace-filled life is passive and lazy. On the contrary, living *from* your connection to God and *from* Jesus' finished work is a life filled with activity, adventure, battles, and good works.

You already know that the writer of Hebrews used the Israelites' entrance into the Promised Land as a metaphor for living the abundant life of New Covenant grace. You also know that God even called living in the Promised Land a form of rest (see Psalm 95:11, Hebrews 3:11). But here's what I want you to think about.

The generation of Israelites that did ultimately cross over into Canaan didn't just get to the other side of the river and sling hammocks between the trees and start napping. No! There were cities to take and enemies to defeat and giants to slay and farms to operate. There was much to accomplish, and yet…God described this new life as rest. Why?

Because all of that activity was meant to be *from*, not *for*. Through both Moses and Joshua, God had said, "I've given you this land. It's yours. Now go take possession of it." All the activity awaiting them on the other side of the river was to be done *from* what God had promised. Done in faith because a faithful God had said it was theirs. Put another way, God didn't say, "Go conquer that land and I'll let you keep it." No, both their confidence and their obedience were an outgrowth of hearing what God had said He'd already done. It was a finished work, so they could rest in it. All that remained to do was walk out the implications.

> Both their confidence and their obedience were an outgrowth of hearing what God had said He'd already done.

Good works, as opposed to dead works, are very important because the Bible makes it clear there are rewards in heaven. Let me share a few verses that let us know that.

Since you call on him as your heavenly Father, the impartial Judge *who judges according to each one's works*, live each day with holy awe and reverence throughout your time on earth. (1 Peter 1:17 TPT, emphasis added)

For the Son of Man will come in the glory of His Father with His angels, and then He will *reward each according to his works*. (Matthew 16:27, emphasis added)

And behold, I am coming quickly [this is Jesus speaking], *and My reward is with Me, to give to every one according to his work*. (Revelation 22:12, emphasis added)

Now, this is not a contradiction to anything we've learned about grace, *if* you understand the difference between dead works and good works.

Dead works don't earn you heavenly rewards. Whatever rewards you do get from dead works, if any, are shallow, fleeting, and in this life only. We can see this difference in some comments Jesus made about the Pharisees. (By the way, the Pharisees were the kings of dead works.)

"Take heed that you do not do your charitable deeds before men, to be seen by them. Otherwise you have no reward from your Father in heaven. Therefore, when you do a charitable deed, do not sound a trumpet before you as the hypocrites do in the synagogues and in the streets, that they may have glory from men. Assuredly, I say to you, *they have their reward*. But when you do a charitable deed, do not let your left hand know what your right hand is doing, that your charitable deed may be in secret; and *your Father who sees in secret will Himself reward you openly*." (Matthew 6:1–4, emphasis added)

A few verses later in that same chapter, Jesus says:

Do not lay up for yourselves treasures on earth, where moth and rust destroy and where thieves break in and steal; *but lay up for yourselves treasures in heaven,* where neither moth nor rust destroys and where thieves do not break in and steal. (Matthew 6:19–20, emphasis added)

Please note that Jesus didn't say, "Store up for my Father and me... We're experiencing a recession here in heaven and need some additional funding." No, He said "Store up *for yourselves* treasure in heaven."

Clearly, there are rewards in heaven, and here on earth, for doing good works and making godly choices in your behavior. But here's the thing. If you don't understand grace, you'll slip into doing those works and (trying) to make godly choices in an effort to qualify for your life-connection to God. You'll invariably end up struggling to earn what can only be received as a gift. But if you understand that by grace, you have an unearned, undeserved, unmerited connection to God that stands solely in Jesus' righteousness and what Jesus earned, deserved, and merited, then you'll find yourself both more motivated to do good works and more empowered to do good works. The same is true with your moral choices. Your enjoyment of God and His presence will begin to change your desires and give you the ability to abstain from behaviors that willpower and self-discipline couldn't touch.

Abiding in God is the key to a lifestyle of laying up treasure in heaven. This—abiding in God—is the key to living a life that gets rewarded. That's the clear message of 1 John 2:28:

And now, little children, *abide in Him,* that when He appears, we may *have confidence and not be ashamed* before Him at His coming. (emphasis added)

BY GRACE: BETTER WORKS

This may be a shocking concept to you, but at Jesus' return, some believers will have confidence, but others will experience varying degrees of shame. What will be the difference? According to this verse, the difference is whether or not they pursued a lifestyle of *abiding in Him*. And as we've already seen, you're much more prone to approach and fellowship with your heavenly Father if you've grounded your heart and identity in the biblical reality of grace and the gift of righteousness. It is those who remain in the wilderness of dead works, prideful legalism, and performance-based approval who never have confidence before God in this life. And if you don't have confidence before God now, when He is invisible, how can you possibly expect to have confidence when you're standing face-to-face with God the Son?

Yet the goodness of the Good News just keeps getting better and better. In Jesus, we have a better husband, a better righteousness, a better rest, and now you know that even our works are better, and produce better rewards. Yet we haven't even gotten to perhaps the best news of all.

PART 3

SONS AND DAUGHTERS, PERIOD.

CHAPTER 14

A SHEPHERD. A SEARCHER. A FATHER.

It may be one of the most widely known of all Jesus' parables. Most people who have never attended a church in their lifetimes understand the reference "prodigal son," even though few of them could give you an accurate definition of the word *prodigal*. (By the way, it means a person who spends money recklessly.)

This entire next part of the book will draw on truths from this familiar story. Come to think of it, perhaps it's *too* familiar. What if familiarity has caused you to miss some powerful insights in this parable? What if it holds the key that could completely alter the course of your life? It very well may. So get ready to see it with fresh eyes. But first, allow me to give you a little context and perspective. Why did Jesus tell this story? What prompted it?

We find it in the fifteenth chapter of Luke right behind two other shorter parables. The fact is, Jesus fired off those three parables in response to a complaint He received.

Yes, Jesus got complaints. Lots of them. All leaders do. This truth reminds me of a story I heard about a monk who joined a monastery that enforced a vow of silence for the first five years of residence. The oath allowed the monks there to say two words, one time each year. After his first full year in the monastery, the abbot came to this new monk and said, "Is there anything you'd like to say?" The monk thought for a moment and said, "Food. Rotten." The abbot looked into the matter and discovered the monastery kitchen had indeed been serving spoiled food consistently. So he ordered improvements in sanitation and quality in the kitchen.

Another year passed and the abbot came to the monk once again to hear the man's precious two words. This time the monk said, "Blankets. Thin." The abbot again looked into the matter and found that the monk was telling the truth. The blankets in the unheated quarters of the monks were pitifully thin and full of holes. So he upgraded all the blankets.

Another year passed and the monk's annual opportunity to speak came around. This time the monk, with sadness in his face, said, "Must. Leave." Upon hearing this, the abbot relied, "That's fine with me. You've done nothing but complain since you got here."

Yes, Jesus got complaints and criticism all the time. And one complaint in particular prompted him to deliver three parables in rapid succession—boom, boom, boom. Here's that complaint:

Then all the tax collectors and the sinners drew near to Him to hear Him. And *the Pharisees and scribes complained*, saying, "This Man receives sinners and eats with them." (Luke 15:-1–2, emphasis added)

In the eyes of some, Jesus was talking to and eating with the wrong kinds of people. He got this complaint a lot. In fact, ten chapters earlier in Luke, Jesus got the very same criticism from the very same crowd. His reply back then was, "Those who are well have no need of a physician, but those who are sick" (Luke 5:31). But this time His response is far more comprehensive. He responds by telling three illustrative stories. Stories of a lost sheep, a lost coin, and a lost son. The star of each parable is a searcher—a shepherd, a woman, a father. All three reveal the heart of our heavenly Father for lost and wayward humanity.

When Jesus arrived on the scene, there were basically three types of Jews living in Israel—the extremely devout (like the Pharisees and scribes), the moderately devout (like the fishermen Jesus called to be His disciples), and the not-devout-at-all. We see something very similar among Jewish people in our day. You see the Ultra-Orthodox who take extreme care to observe every aspect of rabbinic teaching, down to the tiniest detail. But you also see many Jewish people who are moderately observant. And you have completely secular Jews, many of whom don't believe in God at all, yet still take pride in their ethnic heritage.

So as Jesus visited the towns and villages of Israel, He'd teach in the synagogues to reach the observant, but He also walked the highways and byways to reach those who had given up on Law keeping out of frustration, discouragement, or shame. The message for both groups was the same: Repent, for the arrival of the kingdom is right around the corner. *This* is the context of the religious elites' complaint that Jesus was conversing and dining with "sinners." I mention all of this because it bears directly on the parable of the prodigal son and the two other parables Jesus told with it in response to that complaint.

He begins with the parable of the lost sheep. You no doubt know it. Jesus asks the complainers a hypothetical question. "What man of you, having a hundred sheep, if he loses one of them, does not leave the ninety-nine in the wilderness, and go after the one which is lost until he finds it?" (Luke 15:4) Jesus goes on to describe a good shepherd who firmly but lovingly secures the lost sheep and brings it back to the safety of the fold. And once that is done, he throws a party so he and his friends can rejoice at the recovery of this precious asset. Just to make sure His listeners don't miss His point, Jesus provides the interpretation and application of His illustration: "I say to you that likewise there will be more joy in heaven over one sinner who repents than over ninety-nine just persons who need no repentance" (v. 7). When I read these words of Jesus, I can't help but think of an instance in which Jesus plainly stated that His sole mission before going to the cross was to reach "the lost sheep of the house of Israel" (Matthew 15:24).

Yes, on a future Passover weekend He would make a way for *all* the nations of the world to be reconnected to God. But before lying down on that cross, it seems Jesus had another mission: calling wayward sons and daughters of Abraham (including hypocritical Pharisees) to renewed faithfulness to the spirit of the Old, so they would have hearts to receive the New when it came pouring out of heaven on the Day of Pentecost. In other words, before Jesus began the priestly business of mediating a New Covenant between humanity and a God who "so loved the world," He first had a prophetic role to play. A gracious, patient, long-suffering God had raised up one final prophet, exclusively for "the house of Israel."

Jesus follows this "lost sheep" illustration with one about a woman who had lost one coin of the ten she possessed. Her frantic, exhaustive search for the coin reveals that it was precious to her. In fact, it represented a full tenth of her wealth. Like the shepherd in the previous story, the finding of the coin resulted in great rejoicing and a party to celebrate. And again, Jesus makes sure nobody misses His meaning: "Likewise, I say to you, there is joy in the presence of the angels of God over one sinner who repents" (Luke 15:10).

Please note that *repentance* is the objective here. It's the *repentance* that produces the rejoicing in heaven. Many in our culture today try to exploit Jesus' willingness to associate with sinners by turning it into some sort of endorsement, accepting and approving of sinful lifestyles and choices. (Remember, sin is always either self-destructive, others-destructive, or society-destructive.) When believers, in love, try to stand against cultural trends that we know are damaging in this way, we're often accused of being intolerant or hateful. "Jesus ate with tax-gatherers and sinners" is trotted out as a club with which to beat believers for resisting whatever harmful cultural trend is the flavor of the day. That is not a valid takeaway from this passage. Yes, God meets us where we are, but He does not leave us where we are. Engagement does not equal endorsement. Real love will not allow someone to remain in a place that is self-destructive or hurtful to others. Which brings us to our story of a rich kid who ended up in a pigsty.

> Yes, God meets us where we are, but He does not leave us where we are.

The third illustration Jesus gives is His longest and most detailed. It is the powerful narrative that will inform the chapters to come. But for now, let us just note that at its center lies a father with a broken heart. Yet it is a heart filled with hope.

Before we dive in, let me point out one more thing about these three remarkable parables. As I mentioned, Jesus chose as His lead characters: a shepherd, a woman, and a father. Let's think about those three choices for just a moment.

On more than one occasion, Jesus referred to Himself as a shepherd. He declared to His disciples: "I am the good shepherd. The good shepherd gives His life for the sheep" (John 10:11). Is it possible that Jesus has Himself, God the Son, in mind in the first of these three parables?

And what of the parable of the lost coin? He describes a woman who searches. On more than one occasion the Scriptures reveal a "searching" role for the Holy Spirit. For example, Romans 8:27 says, "Now He who searches the hearts knows what the mind of the Spirit is, because He makes intercession for the saints according to the will of God." And 1 Corinthians 2:10 says, "But God has revealed them to us through His Spirit. For the Spirit searches all things, yes, the deep things of God."

Now, the Bible consistently uses masculine pronouns (*He* and *Him*) to refer to the Holy Spirit. Nevertheless, there are Scriptures that also suggest some feminine attributes. In the opening words of the Bible, we see the Spirit of God moving or hovering over the face of the deep (see Genesis 1:2). The Hebrew word translated "hovering" there is a picture-word that suggests a mother bird hovering or fluttering over her nest. Numerous Scriptures speak of the Holy Spirit having a birthing or life-giving function. For example, Jesus told Nicodemus that it was necessary to be born once of a woman but a second time by the Spirit.

I have no intention of taking this too far, but just allow me to suggest that Jesus may have God the Holy Spirit, the searcher, in view in His story about the woman searching for a lost coin.

Finally, and most obviously, Jesus' third story stars a "father." We're about to dive into that one, but for now just consider this.

In one short response to criticism about engaging with sinners, Jesus may very well have depicted God the Son, God the Holy Spirit, and God the Father all passionately involved in seeking and saving "that which was lost" (see Luke 19:10). All of the Godhead longs to save. To rescue. To restore. No wonder the angels rejoice over just one!

> All of the Godhead longs to save. To rescue. To restore. No wonder the angels rejoice over just one!

The father in Jesus' parable has two very different sons. Yet they both had the same problem. Neither son understood what it meant to be a "son" of a good father. Do you? Well, you're about to!

CHAPTER 15

TWO SONS. ONE PROBLEM.

If Hollywood was making a movie based on the parable of the prodigal son, there would be two juicy roles and one *so-so* role. All the actors would be hoping to be cast as either the prodigal or the father. No one would want to be stuck with the part of the *other* brother. He wouldn't even appear in the movie until the very end. And let's be honest, the character is kind of a jerk. Here's the thing: Despite the limited screen time, there is much life-giving truth to be gleaned from the other brother. In fact, the whole story is rich with spiritual insights. So pull up a chair and let me help you see this familiar parable with fresh eyes.

Now, I've lived in Texas almost all my life. It's a big state with some enormous cattle ranches. Some span hundreds of thousands of acres. Visit a large, working cattle ranch and you'll notice something. You'll see the spacious main house where the owner of the ranch and his family live. But invariably, there will be other residential buildings. You'll find a much more modest home for the ranch foreman—the supervisor of all the ranch hands. And you'll find one or more bunkhouses where those ranch hands sleep at night. The ranch hands get regular pay plus a place to sleep and three meals a day. It's not a bad life. But it is nothing like the life experienced by the sons and daughters of the owner of the ranch, even though the children of the ranch owner participate in the same hard work as the hired help. In fact, if you were watching the operation of the ranch on a typical day, you would be hard-pressed to pick out which were sons and daughters and which were employees.

This is very much the situation Jesus envisions in his third parable. Like the previous two, it is given as both an answer and a rebuke to the critical Pharisees and scribes who didn't like Jesus' habit of engaging with people who had abandoned the Jewish faith.

Just in case you're not intimately acquainted with the story as Jesus told it, let's examine it, piece by piece. From The Passion Translation:

> Then Jesus said, "Once there was a father with two sons. The younger son came to his father and said, 'Father, don't you think it's time to give me my share of your estate?'" (Luke 15:11–12a)

It's difficult for the modern, Western mind to understand just how insulting this younger son's request really was in that time and place. It was sort of like coming to your father and saying, "You're taking too long to die, Dad. So, can we just pretend like you're already dead?" It simply wasn't done. According to the norms of culture, the father would have been justified in disinheriting his son completely. But instead we see:

> It's difficult for the modern, Western mind to understand just how insulting this younger son's request really was in that time and place.

"So the father went ahead *and distributed between the two sons* their inheritance." (v. 12b, emphasis added)

We're only in the opening sentences of this parable yet we've already glimpsed the gracious nature of this father's heart. But please notice something else. He doesn't just give the younger son his share. (By the way, that share would have been about half of the older brother's share. Traditionally, the eldest son inherited a double portion relative to all other brothers.) As Jesus tells it, the father gives *both* sons their inheritance. As the New King James puts it, "So he divided to them his livelihood." The Greek word translated "livelihood" there is *bios* (the root of our word *biology*), and it literally means "life." Jesus is telling us that the father willingly gave his whole life, his life's work, and did so for both sons. Of course, the two men responded very differently. The older son remained at home. And...

"Shortly afterward, the younger son packed up all his belongings and traveled off to see the world. He journeyed to a far-off land where he soon wasted all he was given in a binge of extravagant and reckless living. With everything spent and nothing left, he grew hungry, because there was a severe famine in that land." (Luke 15:13–14)

You know the result. Anything described in Israel as a "far-off land" would obviously be a pagan nation. So the young man had not only walked away from his father's house but also walked away from his father's *faith*. He quickly squandered his wealth, ending up broke and in the middle of a famine to boot. So out of the kind of desperation that only extreme hunger can produce, the young man hired on as the lowest of the low-on-the-pecking-order hands at, of all places for a Jewish boy, a pig farm. But on this ranch, there is no bunkhouse and no mess hall. He's sleeping under the stars and eating whatever the pigs are given.

"Humiliated, the son finally realized what he was doing, and he thought, 'There are many workers at my father's house who have all the food they want with plenty to spare. They lack nothing. Why am I here dying of hunger, feeding these pigs and eating their slop? I want to go back home to my father's house, and I'll say to him, "Father, I was wrong. I have sinned against you. I'll never again be worthy to be called your son. Please, Father, just treat me like one of your employees."' So the young son set off for home." (v. 17–20a)

Here are a few things to note about those verses. The young man realized that being a servant in his gracious father's house was far better than being a slave in a pagan land. He assumed he had forfeited any hope of returning to his previous status as a son of the owner, but held out a glimmer of hope of at least being taken on as a hired hand. So he began rehearsing his sales pitch far in advance of arriving back home.

As you know, what follows is one of the most moving and stunning depictions in all of Scripture. Jesus—more intimately acquainted with God's Father-heart than any human being that has ever walked the planet—tells His listeners:

"From a long distance away, his father saw him coming, dressed as a beggar, and great compassion swelled up in his heart for his son who was returning home. The father raced out to meet him, swept him up in his arms, hugged him dearly, and kissed him over and over with tender love." (v. 20b)

The returning son immediately launched into his rehearsed speech but...

"The father interrupted and said, 'Son, you're home now!' Turning to his servants, the father said, 'Quick, bring me the best robe, my very own robe, and I will place it on his shoulders. Bring the ring, the seal of sonship, and I will put it on his finger. And bring out the best shoes you can find for my son. Let's prepare a great feast and celebrate. For my beloved son was once dead, but now he's alive! Once he was lost, but now he is found!' And everyone celebrated with overflowing joy." (v. 21b–24)

There is so much rich truth to unpack in these verses, but I will wait to do so until the next few chapters. For now, let's just take in the final scene in this movie screenplay written by our Redeemer:

"Now, the older son was out working in the field when his brother returned, and as he approached the house, he heard the music of celebration and dancing. He called over one of the servants and asked, 'What's going on?' The servant replied, 'It's your younger brother. He's returned home and your father is throwing a party to celebrate his homecoming.' The older son became angry and refused to go in and celebrate. So his father came out and pleaded with him, 'Come and enjoy the feast with us!' The son said, 'Father, listen!

How many years have I worked like a slave for you, performing every duty you've asked as a faithful son? And I've never once disobeyed you. But you've never thrown a party for me because of my faithfulness. Never once have you even given me a goat that I could feast on and celebrate with my friends as this son of yours is doing now. Look at him! He comes back after wasting your wealth on prostitutes and reckless living, and here you are throwing a great feast to celebrate—for him!' The father said, 'My son, you are always with me by my side. Everything I have is yours to enjoy. It's only right to rejoice and celebrate like this, because your brother was once dead and gone, but now he is alive and back with us again. He was lost, but now he is found!' " (v. 25–31)

Again, as with the previous two parables, the story ends with celebration and rejoicing at the return of what had been lost. And again, there is so much gold to be mined from these carefully chosen words of Jesus. We're about to unearth a lot of it in the next few chapters. But for now, here is what I want you to see. In this story, neither son understood his position with their father.

The younger son believed he had forfeited his sonship by insulting his father, taking a third of his estate, and turning his back on his father's faith. But he was wrong! He may have squandered his inheritance, but he was still just as much a son of this gracious and merciful father as he was the day he was born. The younger man's behavior did not, indeed could not, change the fundamental fact that he was a son. It's clear this younger man had

> The younger man's behavior did not, indeed could not, change the fundamental fact that he was a son.

vastly underestimated two things: (1) the depth of the father's love, and (2) the unbreakable nature of their relational bond.

The elder brother's resentful response and subsequent words reveal that he didn't understand his sonship status, either! His father loved him every bit as much as he loved his brother. This father was clearly generous, kindhearted, and eager to bless. And yet the older son's angry words to his father reveal that he believed he needed to earn and merit and deserve anything the father gave him, much as would a hired servant. Look again:

> "The son said, 'Father, listen! How many years have I worked like a slave for you, performing every duty you've asked as a faithful son? And I've never once disobeyed you. But you've never thrown a party for me because of my faithfulness. Never once have you even given me a goat that I could feast on and celebrate with my friends as this son of yours is doing now.'" (v. 29)

You will recall that the father had previously divided his estate between *both* brothers. Which is why the father could rightly respond by saying, "Everything I have is yours to enjoy." The older son need not wait until the death of the father to enjoy his inheritance. It was available to him now along with the blessing of connection to his living, loving father. What's more, the father had clearly delegated administrative authority to his sons. The older son could have accessed any of the ranch's resources at any time.

The older son could have accessed any of the ranch's resources at any time. Yet he continued to operate like a hired hand.

Yet he continued to operate like a hired hand. And to operate as if his father was hard and stingy, rather than kind and generous. This, too, was an insult to the father. He, too, had vastly underestimated the depth of the father's love and the unbreakable strength of the father-child relational bond.

It's important to understand that many of the Bible's prophecies and parables have a dual fulfillment. In other words, there is an immediate, relevant meaning for the hearers at the time the prophecy is given or the parable is told, yet there is often a second, broader fulfillment for a later time, and this one is no exception.

Remember, Jesus delivered the three parables—the lost sheep, the lost coin, and the lost son—in response to criticism from the Pharisees and scribes about His outreach to those who had abandoned the Old Testament / Old Covenant system, specifically the "tax collectors and sinners." So the immediate meaning of the prodigal son parable would have been clear to everyone within earshot. The prodigal son (like the lost coin and the lost sheep) represented those who had given up on trying to remain faithful to the Old Covenant laws and regulations. Like the younger son, they might have believed they had long since forfeited their right to connection to God and to a form of righteousness through the feasts and festivals of Israel such as the Day of Atonement. But Jesus was telling them they were wrong! Reconnection to God via the commonwealth of Israel was waiting for them. The Father who entered into covenant with them through Moses was still standing on the porch waiting for them to come home. And as the urgency of Jesus' prophetic preaching and teaching revealed, that homecoming was increasingly urgent and vital. Judgment was coming to the House of Israel within a single generation. The end of that old system was near. And something very new and very much better was coming.

Jesus' listeners would also likely have seen a clear reference to the scribes and Pharisees in Jesus' characterization of the angry, resentful older brother. His point was that they, too, had lost their way. Somewhere along the line they had substituted performance for faith—specifically faith in the Day of Atonement sacrifice to cover their sins and provide a form of righteousness for a year. Instead, they, like the rich young ruler, had managed to convince themselves and others that their righteousness came from slavish, obsessive, meticulous, adherence to the regulatory laws of the Torah. This is precisely why Paul spends a significant chunk of the book of Romans explaining that righteousness before God has always come by faith, not works. And that even Father Abraham's righteousness came simply because he believed God. Yes, works and obedience are natural by-products or outgrowths of faith. But it is faith that is the key. Obedience *reveals* a heart of faith, but it can never be a substitute for it.

> Obedience *reveals* a heart of faith, but it can never be a substitute for it.

Yet like the older brother in Jesus' tale, the Pharisees failed to understand the heart of God and His core reason for entering into covenant with them. That reason? Relationship! At some point after the seventy years of captivity in Babylon, Israel's religious establishment had lost the plot. And there they were...angry and resentful that Jesus, on behalf of His Father, was welcoming the prodigals of Israel back into connection with Him if they were willing to return. The fullest expression of that connection could come only after Jesus completed His priestly, sacrificial work. But returning to the true spirit (not the letter) of the Old Covenant seems to have been a key part of that journey.

That was the first, initial fulfillment and meaning of Jesus' parable. But as I mentioned, there is a broader, longer application. An application that is profoundly relevant for you and me, for we, too, have been cast in a role in this epic love story. As we're about to see, many believers are unwittingly playing the role of the older brother. But an understanding of grace puts us squarely into the shoes of the prodigal. And like every other part of the gospel, this contains better news than our minds can comprehend, or our hearts can grasp.

CHAPTER 16

YOUR ROBE

You'll find many fascinating themes and threads in the Bible. We've already seen that one theme is seeds and a Seed. You now know the whole story of God's plan of redemption can be told through the Bible's mentions of seeds. Shepherds-and-sheep stands as another thread. It's remarkable how many key individuals in God's plan of redemption spent time tending sheep or goats. Threshing floors is another recurring piece of imagery in the Bible. It makes a fascinating study to see all the times a threshing floor for wheat or barley makes an appearance in the grand narrative of Scripture.

Here's one more: robes. Think about all the places robes or body-covering garments appear in the amazing storyline of Scripture. In the opening chapters of Genesis, we see fallen Adam and Eve frantically trying to cover their freshly realized nakedness with sewn-together fig leaves. Their compassionate Creator knows these are inadequate. He also knows that without the shedding of blood there is no remission of sin (see Hebrews 9:22). So He personally slays some of His own created creatures and fashions covering garments for the couple.

But a survey of the Bible reveals that robes do more than just cover. In the ancient world of the Bible, robes designated status and authority. Here are just a few examples of many I could mention.

Remember Joseph and his coat of many colors gifted to him by his father, Jacob? That's actually a faulty translation in the King James Version of the original Hebrew phrase in Genesis 37:3. A better translation would be "full-length tunic" or, as one Messianic-Jewish translation of the Bible, the Tree of Life Version, renders it, "a long-sleeved tunic." In other words, from among Jacob's twelve sons, he singled out Joseph to receive a full-length robe that signified his special place in his father's heart. That this was the case is made evident by the reaction of the brothers in the very next verse:

> When his brothers saw that their father loved him more than all his brothers, they hated him and could not speak to him in shalom. (Genesis 37:4 TLV)

Later, when God was establishing the Mosaic Covenant with the Israelite tribes, God gave detailed instructions about what the High Priest was to wear as he ministered in the Holy Place and especially in the Most Holy Place, also known as the Holy of Holies. This included a white linen robe and a tunic of royal blue or purple.

Everything about the priestly coverings and the Holy of Holies was profoundly meaningful and symbolic. I won't take the time to go into detail here, but a study of this reveals that the Holy of Holies was a temporary place on earth that re-created the setting of Adam back in the garden, before sin and the Fall. The ceiling of the chamber was painted like a starry sky, because Adam lived under an open heaven. The seven-branched menorah, or candlestick, was designed as a stylized almond tree symbolizing the Tree of Life in the center of the garden. And God ordered the High Priest's garments to be made of linen rather than wool for a specific reason: The priest was not to wear anything that would make him sweat (see Ezekiel 44:18). What's wrong with a little sweat? It was part of the curse that resulted from the Fall!:

In the sweat of your face you shall eat bread till you return to the ground, for out of it you were taken... (Genesis 3:19a)

Once each year, the High Priest would become, for a few hours, the original Adam before the Fall when, clothed in nothing but righteousness, he could be in God's presence. For fifteen centuries he would serve as an annual forerunner, pointing to the day when another, final "Adam" would arrive to make a way for any willing man or woman to return to that garden of rest and delight to enjoy fellowship with God every day.

There are so many other examples I could mention, including the scene in 1 Samuel 18 wherein Jonathan, the son of King Saul, gives his royal robe to David as part of a covenant ceremony, foreshadowing that David, not Jonathan, would one day become the next king of the united tribes of Israel.

But the robe I must now point you to is the one Jesus was wearing the night He was arrested. The nineteenth chapter of John reveals that Jesus wasn't given a robe. No, the sinless, utterly righteous Son of God was stripped of His. For His trial, the rightful Prince of Heaven was briefly given a purple robe, but only in mockery. This, too, was stripped from Him so He could hang naked before a taunting, horrified public. As He hung there, bleeding, Roman soldiers gambled for His seamless robe in fulfillment of ancient prophecy.

Do you see the importance in the light of all we've just seen about the significance of robes? They can signify status, office, and authority, as with a king. They can also signify righteousness, as with the High Priest. And as with Joseph, a robe can be an outward visible sign that the wearer is loved.

Do you now see that Jesus was all of these things—the King of Kings, utterly righteous, unspeakably loved by His heavenly Father, and more—and yet on the cross He was stripped of them to make it possible for you and me to receive them as a gift? The stripping of Jesus of everything, including His robe, is just one aspect of the reality that, on the cross, Jesus bore everything mankind forfeited in the Fall so we, through His death, might be completely restored. Oh yes, robes are meaningful.

This brings us back to the symbols Jesus chose to use in His telling of story of the prodigal son. Here's a quick reminder:

> "And the son said to him, 'Father, I have sinned against heaven and in your sight, and am no longer worthy to be called your son.' But the father said to his servants, *'Bring out the best robe and put it on him, and put a ring on his hand and sandals on his feet.* And bring the fatted calf here and kill it, and let us eat and be merry; for this my son was dead and is alive again; he was lost and is found.' And they began to be merry." (Luke 15:21–24, emphasis added)

Jesus mentioned three items—a robe, ring, and sandals. This is no accident. Jesus chose every word of that parable with intentionality and Holy Spirit guidance. We'll examine all three in time, but given everything we've just learned, let's focus on the robe for the balance of this chapter.

Please recall the previous chapter where we saw how the returning younger brother believed he had forfeited his standing as son by insulting and shaming his father, squandering a huge chunk of his father's life's work, and abandoning his father's faith. The only way his mind could conceive of returning to the shelter and provision of the ranch was to return as a servant. In other words, to begin to *earn* anything and everything he hoped to receive.

We also saw he was wrong. Wrong about everything.

As we defined grace in the opening chapters of this book, we discovered that God's grace-gifts are always and only *unearned*. If you will only grasp this truth, plant it in the good soil of your heart, and let it take root so deeply that it begins to form your sense of identity, it will change everything about your life going forward. Yet so many of God's sons and daughters will say, if asked, "Yes, my standing with God is a *gift*," while all the time behaving, thinking, and operating as if it's *earned*. Your actions always reveal what you *really* believe.

Grasping this truth—that what God desires to give you is 100 percent *gift* and 0 percent *earned*—will change everything about:

- the way you see yourself;
- the way you treat yourself;
- the way you see others;
- the way you treat others;
- and most of all, the way you see, approach, and connect with your heavenly Father.

The younger son had been nothing but arrogant, foolish, selfish, and sinful. *Depraved* is actually a better word for his lifestyle. So please tell me what he had done to *earn* the three gifts lavished upon him by his father upon his return. The clear answer is nothing. In fact, if earning had anything at all to do with the bestowing of these gifts, this young man would have earned rebuke and rejection.

Please note for a moment what this young man said in the opening of his rehearsed speech. It's quite revealing: "I am no longer worthy to be called your son..." (v. 19) Do you see it? The words *no longer worthy* imply that he once thought himself worthy. His mindset was that good behavior—doing all the "dos" and avoiding all the "don'ts"—qualified him to be called a son. Given that paradigm, it makes perfect sense that he thought his bad behavior had then disqualified him from sonship. He seemed to think that if he had stayed at home and done all the right things, he would have continued to *deserve* or *merit* his place at the table with his father. This reveals a fundamental lack of understanding of the grace-based nature of fatherhood and sonship. (Please understand that here and through the rest of this book, I am using the terms *son* and *sonship* in a generic sense that embraces both males and females. Jesus used sons to make a point with this parable, but the truths it contains apply with equal relevance and power to both sons and daughters of God.)

We're going to examine the stunning, glorious reality of our adoption as children of God in an upcoming chapter, but for now just let me ask: How often do we, as beloved sons and daughters of a gracious heavenly Father, bring this same mindset into church on the weekend?

If you've had a bad-performance week—a stretch of days in which you've repeatedly overslept your quiet-time appointment, yelled at the kids, hurt your spouse's feelings, and done several other "don'ts" that you'd vowed to stop doing—you walk into church carrying a load of shame and heavy sense of disqualification. Your spiritual posture is, "I'm not worthy to be called your son." If, on the other hand, you're walking into worship after a stretch of days in which you have performed pretty well, it's tempting to think you may have earned or merited some confidence before God.

Let me be clear. If either is your mindset, you're wrong. Your standing or position as a child of the Father is not in any way related to your performance. Once again, the best-performance day you've ever had in your life is the equivalent of filthy, smelly rags in comparison with the righteousness necessary to be reconnected to intimate relationship with a holy God.

What is the solution, then? Well, that question brings us back to the first of those three gifts the father lavished on the wayward son—a robe.

As we've already seen, the High Priest's robes of linen pointed both backward and forward. They pointed backward to a time before the Fall in which Adam and Eve, in complete innocence and purity, had free, no-sweat access to God's presence and fellowship. And at the same time, they depicted and foreshadowed a time when the ultimate High Priest, Jesus, would make a way for us to be clothed or robed in His own innocence and purity. In His righteousness. And in those spotless robes we now have been restored to free and unhindered access to the Father's presence once more. The prophet Isaiah foresaw this:

I will greatly rejoice in the LORD, my soul shall be joyful in my God; for He has clothed me with the garments of salvation, *He has covered me with the robe of righteousness*... (Isaiah 61:10a, emphasis added)

Another Old Testament passage foreshadowed this miracle, too. We find it in the book of Zechariah, Chapter 3. This is a prophecy involving a High Priest named Joshua (not *that* Joshua; this one lived nearly a thousand years later, after the Jews returned to Israel following seventy years of exile in Babylon).

God gave Zechariah a prophetic vision in which he saw an angel standing with the High Priest Joshua in his sacred priestly garments, but they were filthy. The linen that was supposed to be brilliantly white was covered in nasty muck. This represented the reality that over the centuries in Israel, the priesthood had become corrupted. The nation had repeatedly wandered away from God and the stipulations of the Mosaic Covenant, and often the priests had led the way. Read about the priests Hophni and Phineas in 1 Samuel 2 and 3. These two sons of the High Priest Eli were as debauched and immoral as you can possibly imagine. And that was pretty early in Israel's history. Around Zechariah's time, the entire book of Malachi was written essentially as an indictment by God of the Levitical priesthood.

So what about Zechariah's vision of the High Priest Joshua with the unclean priestly garments?

Now Joshua was clothed with filthy garments, and was standing before the Angel. Then He answered and spoke to those who stood before Him, saying, "Take away the filthy garments from him." And to him He said, "See, I have removed

your iniquity from you, and I will clothe you with rich robes."
(Zechariah 3:3–4)

Do you see it? Once again, we see a robe or garments symbolizing a *gift* of purity and righteousness. That's right, a gift! Joshua did nothing to earn or deserve this change of wardrobe. The garments were bestowed solely because the voice of the angel commanded it. As this wasn't just any angel. Look at the two preceding verses:

> Then he showed me Joshua the high priest *standing before the Angel of the LORD*, and Satan standing at his right hand to oppose him. And the LORD said to Satan, "The LORD rebuke you, Satan! The LORD who has chosen Jerusalem rebuke you! Is this not a brand plucked from the fire?" (Zechariah 3:1–2, emphasis added)

It is widely understood that the term *Angel of the Lord* here and elsewhere in the Old Testament refers to God the Son among the three members of the Trinity. In other words, this is Jesus. Another figure is present as well, Satan, doing what he does—opposing and accusing. Please notice that he got rebuked for that!

You need to understand that the enemy of your soul always stands ready to accuse you and point out all the ways you've messed up and fallen short. Yet when you came to Jesus, He was standing by with a command to have your dirty clothes replaced with a spotless, white robe!

> You need to understand that the enemy of your soul always stands ready to accuse you and point out all the ways you've messed up and fallen short.

Is it any wonder that when telling this story of the Prodigal in the presence of the critical, accusatory Pharisees, Jesus chose a robe as the first gift from the father? Jesus knew he was about to go to the cross and bear the penalty and shame for the sins of all mankind. All the filth of all the robes that have ever been or ever would be was about to be laid upon Him.

Yes, the robe presented to the returning prodigal in Jesus' parable certainly represented a complete recognition of his unforfeited status as a son, but it represented far more than that. It looked forward to a soon-coming day when Jesus' own righteousness could be wrapped like a robe around naked sinners like you and I as an utterly unearned gift. This is a clear message Paul is trying to get across to us in Romans Chapters 3, 4, and 5. See this, for example:

> *This righteousness from God comes through faith in Jesus Christ to all who believe.* There is no difference, for all have sinned and fall short of the glory of God, and are justified freely by his grace through the redemption that came by Christ Jesus. (Romans 3:22–24)

Where does righteousness come from? "From God," not our own efforts. *How* does it come? "Through faith"! By *what* are we "justified freely"? "By His grace!"

This couldn't be clearer. Yet the overwhelming temptation is to read these words, say hallelujah!—and then slide right back into thinking, acting, and relating to God as if our connection to Him rose and fell on our own good behavior. Perhaps that's why Paul goes at it from a different angle two chapters later. There, he reminds us that the sin of our ancestor Adam didn't just rob him (and us) of righteousness, but also unleashed some terrible things into the world including death. But that the obedience of a new "Adam"—Jesus—unleashed some things as well:

> For if by the one man's offense death reigned through the one, much more those who receive *abundance of grace and of the gift of righteousness* will reign in life through the One, Jesus Christ. (Romans 5:17, emphasis added)

Through Jesus, "the One," you and I have received two things: (1) an "abundance of grace" and (2) "the gift of righteousness." The *what* of righteousness? The gift! In truth, the second thing (the gift) is evidence of the first thing (the grace). We are wrapped in robes of righteousness because of and through God's infinite, overflowing reservoirs of grace.

Alone, on my knees at a little roadside inn called Jake's Motel, I surrendered my life to Jesus at the age of nineteen. I rose from the shag carpet fully and forever reborn and bound for heaven. But for years I didn't understand the truth about that robe of righteousness. Yes, I understood and gratefully embraced the amazing truth that all my sins were forgiven. What I didn't realize was that, along with my sins, Jesus also took away my shame.

I walked needlessly in shame for years because I still vividly recalled the depth and height of the sin in which I had been involved as a young man. And even after I was saved, I continued to mess up in ways small and large. Of course, I would run to 1 John 1:9 and confess my sin, laying hold of the promise that God would mercifully forgive me and cleanse me of "all unrighteousness." I invariably saw His mercy as washing away my *guilt* but never my *shame*.

Which meant I often felt disqualified from being used by God in any significant way. (Which was a problem, because I knew I had a ministry call on my life!)

Then one day the truth of Jesus' parable broke through my thick noggin and worked its way into my heart. I *got* that what the father of the prodigal did by wrapping his repentant son in that special robe is what my heavenly Father had done for me. It was as if the son had never left at all! I had been—to use a theological term—*justified*. That word means "just as if I'd never sinned at all." Eventually, I realized it was profoundly inappropriate for me to carry around the shame for my sin. Jesus bore my shame on the cross just as surely as He'd born the guilt of my sin.

In the light of that truth, I began to realize that I'm not righteous because I consistently live righteously. No, I live more and more righteously over time because I've been declared righteous. Because I've been wrapped in that robe—been gifted Jesus' own righteousness—I have intimate connection and relationship with God. And that connection causes me to live more and more in alignment with who I already am. The same is true for you. You and I are righteous by the blood of Jesus, even though we don't always live righteously.

> I began to realize that I'm not righteous because I consistently live righteously. No, I live more and more righteously over time because I've been declared righteous.

Many believers have accepted that they have access to God because of the cross. Yet because they're sin-conscious rather than gift-of-righteousness-conscious, they continue to use their amazing gift of access sporadically and sheepishly. They only go to God in a crisis. And when they do go to Him, they slink in on their bellies, weighed down with shame and overwhelming feelings of disqualification.

Here's the thing. In the New Covenant, Jesus' blood doesn't just give us access, it gives us "confident" access:

> Christ Jesus our Lord, in whom we have boldness and access with confidence through faith in Him. (Ephesians 3:11b–12)
>
> For we do not have a High Priest who cannot sympathize with our weaknesses, but was in all points tempted as we are, yet without sin. Let us therefore come boldly to the throne of grace, that we may obtain mercy and find grace to help in time of need. (Hebrews 4:15–16)

No believer carrying around shame is "bold" or "confident" before God. It's unthinkable. Yet according to these verses and others, that is precisely how we're privileged to approach our heavenly Father. It is the way sons and daughters approach a good father, even when they've messed up. Servants, on the other hand, approach with trepidation, fear, and shame.

> No believer carrying around shame is "bold" or "confident" before God. It's unthinkable.

Embracing and internalizing your true identity as a son or daughter, rather than the false identity of a servant, doesn't just happen instantly after reading a few Scriptures, or reading a chapter like this one. It is a *process*. A mind-renewal process. And we know from Romans 12:2 that we are transformed by the renewing of our minds. Regularly and intentionally renewing your mind to the truth about your robe of righteousness will transform you. From the inside out, you'll begin to act righteously because you know you have been declared righteous. Day after day, your actions will begin coming into alignment with your God-declared identity:

Beloved son. Cherished daughter.

Remember this, however. That robe of righteousness wasn't the only gift bestowed upon the returning son. Other gifts are yours, too. It's long past time that you understood them and received them.

CHAPTER 17

YOUR RING

Several years ago, Israeli archaeologists digging on the Temple Mount in an area called David's Citadel came across something truly remarkable. While a scientist was sifting through twenty-five centuries' worth of rubble, something caught his trained eye. A little dusting and cleaning revealed a stone signet ring. At first glance, it seemed similar to the thousands of other ancient signet rings that have been unearthed throughout the Middle East and Mediterranean region over the years.

In case you're unaware, a signet ring is one that bears engraved marks identifying the owner. The Hebrew writing on this ring was engraved in reverse, sometimes called mirror writing. Why? Because these rings would be pressed into soft wax to serve the same function as signatures on contracts do today. The mirror writing on the ring would create a correctly oriented impression on the wax. Kings, lords, and wealthy individuals would have signet rings made for themselves and for those to whom they had delegated the authority to handle their finances or make deals on their behalf.

We see the significance of a signet ring in the Joseph narrative in the book of Genesis:

Then Pharaoh took his signet ring off his hand and put it on Joseph's hand; and he clothed him in garments of fine linen and put a gold chain around his neck. And he had him ride in the second chariot which he had; and they cried out before him, "Bow the knee!" So he set him over all the land of Egypt. (Genesis 41:42–43)

What a vivid picture of how the signet ring symbolically conveys a delegation of authority! A signet ring also makes an appearance in the book of Esther. As wicked Haman is scheming against all the Jewish people living in the kingdom of Persia, he persuades King Ahasuerus to go along with a plan to kill them all. Here is how the king demonstrated his initial agreement with the plan: "So the king took his signet ring from his hand and gave it to Haman..." (Esther 3:10a).

By handing Haman his ring, the king was delegating to Haman royal authority and power.

This is the very type of ring that emerged in the sifter on the Temple Mount. As I said, at first glance, the discovering archaeologist thought this signet ring was a typical one. But further inspection revealed that it was quite special. Tests revealed that the ring dated to a time known as the First Temple Period. The First Temple was the one financed by David, built by Solomon, and destroyed by the Babylonians in 586 B.C.

What blew the minds of the archaeologists was what they found written on the ring in mirror writing once they cleaned it up—a name: ELIHANA BAT GAEL.

Elihana is the feminine version of the name Eli. And as you may know, in Hebrew, *bat* means "daughter of." So the primary inscription on the ring reads, "Elihana, daughter of Gael." The ring also carried the full name of her father, Gael. The story the ring is telling is that more than twenty-five hundred years ago, a Jewish father named Gael had such confidence in his beloved daughter, Elihana, that he gave her a signet ring carrying both of their names. With that ring she carried all the authority of the father himself. She could use that delegated authority—embodied in her possession of that ring—to transact business, make purchases, and enter into contracts on his behalf. This, in a time and part of the world in which women were often treated like children at best and livestock at worst.

Five centuries or more later, in Jesus' day, wealthy Jewish fathers were still using signet rings. Which is why His audience must have immediately grasped the implications of the following detail in Jesus' parable of the prodigal:

"But the father said to his servants, 'Bring out the best robe and put it on him, *and put a ring on his hand* and sandals on his feet.'" (Luke 15:22)

This wasn't a gift of an ornamental piece of jewelry. The father in Jesus' parable was making a clear and unmistakable statement by placing the ring on his son's finger. Again, a ring represents delegated authority. With it, the father is saying, "This is my son, and he is *authorized* to speak for me, to decide for me, and to act for me."

Please note that the English words *authorized* and *authority* share the same root. The Bible has much to say about authority. The

Scriptures make it clear that God is a God of order and hierarchy and process, rather than chaos. Think about it. Before He spoke the universe into existence there were already myriad created angelic beings, and the Scriptures make it clear that those

> The Scriptures make it clear that God is a God of order and hierarchy and process, rather than chaos.

beings were organized into classes and ranks and hierarchies. It is no accident that when Lucifer fell, a third of the angelic host seemingly joined the rebellion and fell with him. This suggests a chain of command. Very few believers have even a minimal understanding of how God works through delegated authority. So before we examine the significance of the gift of that ring, let's get some of that needed understanding.

In the opening chapters of the Bible, we see God delegating authority over Planet Earth to His son and daughter, Adam and Eve (see Genesis 1:28). Looking at the Scriptures as a whole also suggests that Adam's Fall, in some form and to some degree, caused that authority over the earth to be forfeited to God's archenemy, Satan. How do we know this?

For one thing, Jesus himself suggests it on a couple of occasions. On the night of the last supper, Jesus told His disciples, "I will no longer talk much with you, for the ruler of this world is coming, and he has nothing in Me" (John 14:30). The "ruler of this world"? Really? Here's that same verse in the Expanded Bible:

> I will not talk with you much longer, because the ruler [prince] of this world [Satan] is coming. He has no power [no claim/hold; nothing] over me. (John 14:30 EXB)

This translation does a good job of reflecting all the different ways these words of Jesus could be translated from the Greek. The Greek words include *archon* (prince or ruler) and *kosmos* (world, system, or order).

An *archon* was a governmental office holder in the Greek and Roman Empires. This was someone chosen by an emperor to rule over a city or a province. Often such a ruler was a son or relative of the emperor, and thus a "prince." During Jesus' time, there was a related office in the Roman Empire called *tetrarch*, which translates as "ruler of a quarter or one-fourth." The Roman governor who had John the Baptist executed, for instance, was Herod the Tetrarch. The office of *archon* involves authority or rulership that is delegated from the highest ruler.

So we have to take notice when Jesus, just before going to the cross, calls Satan the ruler or prince (*archon*) of this world, or of the systems of this world (*kosmos*). Jesus would do so again later that same night in saying, "the ruler of this world has already been judged" (John 16:11 NLT).

There is one more piece of circumstantial evidence. Do you recall the temptation of Jesus in the wilderness immediately following His baptism? After going forty days without food, Jesus was faced with three fierce temptations. I just want to point out something about the second of these temptations:

> Then the devil, taking Him up on a high mountain, showed Him all the kingdoms of the world in a moment of time. And the devil said to Him, *"All this authority I will give You,* and their glory; *for this has been delivered to me,* and I give it to whomever I wish. Therefore, if You will worship before me, all will be

Yours." And Jesus answered and said to him, "Get behind Me, Satan! For it is written, 'You shall worship the LORD your God, and Him only you shall serve.'" (Luke 4:5–8, emphasis added)

There is much I could say about this, but for now I just want to point out that Satan showed Jesus "all the kingdoms of the world" and then offered to give "all this authority" over them to Jesus in exchange for Jesus' worship. Notice also that Satan describes that authority has having previously "been delivered" to him. Here's my question. These "temptations" of Jesus can only be a truly hard test if they are genuinely tempting, right? Since the first temptation failed, the second one needed to be even *more* tempting than reminding a starving man He could turn stones into bread. If Satan did not, at that moment, have rulership over the kingdoms of the earth, then his offer to Jesus would have been meaningless, and Jesus would have known it. The devil could only offer them to Jesus if they, in some sense, truly had "been delivered" to him.

So how did Satan become, as Jesus called him, the *archon* of this *kosmos*? As I've already suggested, it had to have happened in the Fall. In a very real sense, God had designated Adam His official *archon* for Planet Earth. He had legally and covenantally delegated His sovereign authority to man. God intended man to partner with Him in carrying out His good plans and purposes on this planet.

Here's the thing. God is righteous and holy and good. He doesn't make rules for a system and then ignore them when they get inconvenient. He doesn't establish a covenant then break it when his covenant partner

> God is righteous and holy and good. He doesn't make rules for a system and then ignore them when they get inconvenient.

messes things up or squanders his inheritance. No, He is a Father who keeps covenant to "a thousand generations" (see Exodus 20:6, Deuteronomy 7:9, Psalm 105:8). So only another "Adam" could legally recover what the first Adam had lost. The first Adam, with a full belly, faced a test of obedience in a plush green paradise filled with abundance—and failed. This new Adam, Jesus, faced the same test of obedience but while nearly starving in a harsh, barren wilderness—and passed.

Now think back to what Jesus said about Satan in John 14:30. He said the ruler of this world is coming, "but he has no claim on me." Every single person born after Adam's Fall was born with Satan having some sort of legal, rightful claim on them. With something "in" them (see Colossian 1:13). But not Jesus. The miraculous, brilliantly conceived circumstances of Jesus' birth meant that Satan had nothing in Him.

> The miraculous, brilliantly conceived circumstances of Jesus' birth meant that Satan had nothing in Him.

That would have changed if Jesus had failed the test of obedience. But He didn't!

With all of that in mind, let's contrast Jesus' description of Satan as "the ruler of this world" right *before* the cross, with something Jesus said immediately *after* the cross and His victory over death. He told His disciples:

And Jesus came and spoke to them, saying, *"All authority has been given to Me in heaven and on earth.* Go therefore and make disciples of all the nations, baptizing them in the name of the Father and of the Son and of the Holy Spirit..." (Matthew 28:18–19, emphasis added)

Notice that Jesus included not just "in heaven" but also "on earth" in His proclamation of "all authority." What had changed?

Everything! Paul, who received direct revelation from Jesus Himself, and had even been caught up into the third heaven (the realm where God abides) understood this at a high level. In Colossians Chapter 2 Paul declares that Jesus is "head of all principality and power" (v. 10). And then says:

Having disarmed principalities and powers, He made a public spectacle of them, triumphing over them in it. (v. 15)

The Greek word translated "disarmed" there—*apekduomai*—can mean "disarm" but also has the meaning of "undress" or "strip off."[4] Paul saw that Jesus' victory actually stripped Satan of the robe of authority he had been wearing ever since Adam so foolishly handed it over to him. Jesus had disarmed him of any legal rights where legal control of this planet was concerned. From that moment forward, Satan became an outlaw and a trespasser. A squatter living in a home he no longer had any legal right to occupy. Of course, there's a difference between authority and power. Yes, Jesus stripped Satan of all authority, but our enemy did retain some power—specifically the power to deceive. That's the same power he had before the Fall when Adam and Eve were still the God-ordained *archons* of earth. It's the power he used to con Eve into using her God-given gift of free will to violate God's prohibition of eating from the Tree of the Knowledge of Good and Evil. Deception was Satan's

> Deception was Satan's original power, and it's the one he's left with after being stripped.

original power, and it's the one he's left with after being stripped. He knows that, as he did with Eve, his only play is to deceive us and trick us into using our own God-gifted power of free will against ourselves.

In announcing that all authority in heaven and on earth had been given to Him, Jesus was declaring that the Last Adam had regained what the first Adam had lost. And because of that, everything going forward would be different. Paul has this in mind when he prayed that the believers in Ephesus would have the eyes of their understanding opened to several spiritual realities. One of those realities he mentions is that they would comprehend

what is the exceeding greatness of His power toward us who believe, according to the working of His mighty power which He worked in Christ when He raised Him from the dead and *seated Him at His right hand in the heavenly places, far above all principality and power and might and dominion, and every name that is named, not only in this age but also in that which is to come. And He put all things under His feet, and gave Him to be head over all things* to the church, which is His body, the fullness of Him who fills all in all. (Ephesians 1:19–23, emphasis added)

Everything about those verses speaks of absolute authority. Being seated at God's right hand? Authority. Being seated "far above all principality and power and might and dominion"? Authority. Having a name that is above "every name that is named"? Authority. Having "all things under His feet"? Authority!

The Greek word translated "power" in this passage is *exousia*, a word usually translated "authority" elsewhere in the New Testament. It's the same word Jesus used when He told His disciples that all "authority" in heaven and on earth belonged to Him. What an insult to Jesus' victory it is when we speak and believe and behave as if Satan is still the legal authority in this world. But there's more.

As we've seen, authority can be delegated. When I was a young man in the early years of ministry, I served under a wonderful senior pastor named Olen Griffing. On more than one occasion I heard him say, "When I was younger, I could stop a semi-tractor-trailer truck with one hand." He would then reveal that prior to entering full-time ministry, he was a Texas state trooper. As he explained, in the authority delegated by the State of Texas and symbolized by the badge the state had given him, he could stand in the middle of the highway and hold up one hand and stop any vehicle, including eighteen-wheelers.

Olen once described walking up on a sleeping driver in an illegally parked car. The driver was a huge man with a golf cap pulled down over his eyes. Olen tapped on the half-open window and said, "Sir, you can't park here." The man roused a little and growled, "Who says I can't park here?" Olen said, "The State of Texas says you can't park here." The man sat up, pushed the bill of his cap back, and turned, looking right into Olen's shiny badge. "Yes, sir," the man said quietly as he started up the car. The man recognized authority. No, that authority didn't come from who Olen was or from anything he'd done. It came from the state that issued that badge. The whole State of Texas was behind him when he spoke.

That's delegated authority. Numerous Scriptures make it clear that as born-again believers, we're in Jesus and Jesus is in us. This means that we carry His authority (see Matthew 16:19, Mark 16:17, Luke 9:1, Luke 10:18–19, John 14:12, 2 Corinthians 10:2–5, Ephesians 2:6, and 1 John 4:4). It's not our authority, it's His. Yet, as with Elihana and her father, it's both our name and His name on the signet ring that He's placed on our fingers.

Is it any wonder Jesus had the father of the prodigal placing a ring on his finger in His parable? He knew that one day soon He would make a way for a world full of prodigals, both Jew and Gentile, to come to the Father through Him. And that when they did, the Father would not only wrap them in the robe of His own righteousness, but also place a ring of authority upon their fingers. Delegated authority. That delegation is implied in what follows the word *therefore* in Jesus' "all authority" announcement:

> Then Jesus came to them and said, "All authority in heaven and on earth has been given to me. *Therefore* go and make disciples of all nations, baptizing them in the name of the Father and of the Son and of the Holy Spirit, and teaching them to obey everything I have commanded you. And surely I am with you always, to the very end of the age." (Matthew 28:18–20 NIV, emphasis added)

Do you see it? Jesus says that because he has regained authority over the earth, those who are in Him can "therefore go" into all of *His* world. Here He echoes the marching orders to Adam and Eve back in Genesis, namely, to "be fruitful, multiply, fill the earth, and rule over it" (paraphrasing Genesis 1:28). It's also an echo of God's marching orders to the Israelites as they prepared to enter the Land of Promise. God essentially said, "I've given you this land. Now go and possess it."

Just a few paragraphs ago I mentioned that, prior to the Fall, God had originally intended man to partner with Him in carrying out His good plans and purposes on this planet. Jesus' "all authority" announcement to His disciples, followed by what has come to be called the Great Commission, represents a declaration that the plan is back on!

This brings us to a mind-blowing aspect of this revelation: God has *chosen* to need us. He didn't have to need us to accomplish His will in the earth. He just wanted to! Fathers love to work with their sons and daughters. There is a reason Jesus, when asked for wisdom about how to pray, included the phrase, "Father...your kingdom come, your will be done on earth as it is in heaven" (Matthew 6:10). There is a reason Jesus said, "Most assuredly, I say to you, he who believes in Me, the works that I do he will do also; and greater works than these he will do, because I go to My Father" (John 14:12).

> God has *chosen* to need us. He didn't have to need us to accomplish His will in the earth. He just wanted to!

When you and I, as prodigals, returned to relationship with our heavenly Father, the ring He placed on our fingers was a ring of authority. It has two names on it: your name and Jesus Christ, King of Kings. But this presents a question that has probably already arisen in your mind.

If we have this authority, why do so many Christian lives seem so powerless?

If Jesus has given us "the authority to trample on serpents and scorpions, and over all the power of the enemy, and nothing shall by any means hurt you" (Luke 10:19), why is the devil seemingly running roughshod over so many believers?

There are three things that tend to keep us from walking in the authority that comes with the ring our wonderful Father placed on our fingers. Three things that effectively limit our ability to partner with God in carrying out the King's plans and purposes in the earth.

Would you care to know what those three things are? Let's examine them!

CHAPTER 18

KEYS TO WEARING THE RING

Over in the corner of her drab little room the box sits, sad and neglected. The colorful paper on the lovingly wrapped package has faded from years of exposure to the light. The once-billowing bow of gold ribbon on the top of the parcel now hangs limp and flat. A thin layer of dust covers the top of the present.

The gift from her father arrived years ago yet remains unopened. Things had ended badly between them. In a fit of pride and willfulness, she'd said some things to him she later deeply regretted. A little maturity and life experience ultimately changed her views. As it does for many of us, time had given her some perspective. Nevertheless, a barbed-wire fence of pride and shame keeps her from reconnecting with him. The same barrier keeps unopened the package he sent not long after their angry parting.

What she doesn't know...can't know...is that the gift it holds would have made everything in her life better had she opened it immediately. It would have eased her burdens and protected her from harm. It still can. Yet there it sits. Unopened.

I know the little fictional picture I just painted seems impossibly sad, yet countless believers are just like that woman. I've been like that woman—a recipient of a gift from a loving Father that remained largely unopened and therefore unused. In the early chapters of this book we saw that *grace* implies a gift, and that gifts must be *received* to be activated. Not earned. Not deserved. Not merited. Received. And we saw in the previous chapter that one of the amazing grace-gifts our heavenly Father bestows upon us when we come to Him is a ring of authority, as symbolized in the parable of the prodigal son. Yet no gift unwraps itself.

We saw Jesus' declaration that He'd received "all authority…in heaven and on earth" (Matthew 28:18). He also said He was delegating to His followers "the authority to trample on serpents and scorpions, and over all the power of the enemy," and that "nothing shall by any means hurt" us (Luke 10:19). Throughout the Bible, serpents and scorpions are symbols for demonic powers. So why isn't every Christian on the planet—and by some estimates there are roughly two billion of us—experiencing complete victory over the enemy of their souls? Why don't new believers instantly start walking in all the dominion Adam had before the Fall? Why do some Christians clearly operate in more victory and more breakthrough than others?

> So why isn't every Christian on the planet—and by some estimates there are roughly two billion of us—experiencing complete victory over the enemy of their souls?

These are important questions. And I'm convinced the answers lie in understanding three key attributes or three traits that tend to characterize believers who have fully unwrapped the gift of the ring of authority their heavenly Father provided through Jesus. These are

Christians who wear it with great effectiveness and consistency—pushing back darkness and bringing redemptive hope wherever they go.

First, we've seen from the very opening pages of this book that the principal obstacle to receiving any grace-gift is pride, and that pride is often rooted in insecurity. Pride desperately wants to deserve and merit. As with the woman in the illustration with which I opened this chapter, pride leaves gifts unopened. All of this means that the first common characteristic of those who wear and wield their ring of authority is *humility*. Pride could have kept the prodigal from ever going home. And pride could have kept him from accepting that robe and that ring. Had he insisted on earning or paying back, he would have moved into the bunkhouse with the rest of the hired help and lived like a servant rather than a son. Yet the prodigal in Jesus' story humbly allowed the father to usher him back into the grand owner's house and to seat him at the family table where sumptuous meals were served to sons and daughters.

The New Testament has much to say about the power of humility. Just above I referenced the time Jesus told His disciples that he was delegating to them "the authority to trample on serpents and scorpions, and over all the power of the enemy" (Luke 10:19). That announcement came as the seventy disciples Jesus had sent out in pairs returned jubilantly reporting that even the demons had been subject to them in Jesus' name (v. 17). I chuckle inside every time I read that verse, because the disciples delivered their news as if Jesus would be as shocked by it as they were. It's like they're saying, "Rabbi, you're not going to believe this, but we even had authority over demons!" Jesus' response was, paraphrasing, "Uhhh, yeah. I saw Satan thrown down from heaven and body-slammed to earth.

So…yeah…I've gifted you with authority to walk over all the power of the enemy."

We find more of Jesus' response in the two verses that followed his "serpents and scorpions" statement. Check out verses twenty and twenty-one in The Passion Translation:

"However, your real source of joy isn't merely that these spirits submit to your authority, but that your names are written in the journals of heaven and that you belong to God's kingdom. *This is the true source of your authority.*" Then Jesus, overflowing with the Holy Spirit's joy, exclaimed, "Father, thank you, for you are Lord Supreme over heaven and earth! You have hidden the great revelation of this authority *from those who are proud,* those wise in their own eyes, *and you have shared it with these who humbled themselves.* Yes, Father. This is what pleases your heart: to give these things *to those who are like trusting children.*" (Luke 10:20–21, emphasis added)

Here Jesus first reveals that the source of their authority is that they belong to the kingdom of God. This makes sense when you think about it. When you belong to and represent the King—the One who has all authority—that authority is imputed and imparted to you to some degree. But it was destined to get even better. After the cross, the reality would be that we not only belong to the kingdom but have actually been adopted by the King! (More on that in an upcoming chapter.) Notice what happens next in the passage I just quoted.

Pure, Holy Spirit joy overflows out of Jesus in an eruption of prophetic prayer. "Then Jesus, overflowing with the Holy Spirit's joy, exclaimed, "Father, thank you…" (v. 21 TPT). Pay attention to something Jesus says in the happy song of thanksgiving that followed that "thank you." He is overwhelmed with gratitude that the stunning, ancient secret—that from the very beginning God's plan was to restore divine spiritual authority to humans like you and me—was withheld from the proud. It wasn't those who thought themselves super-smart and highly credentialed that were the first to get a taste of this mind-blowing

> Fishermen, shopkeepers, day laborers, tax collectors, and sheep herders became the first human beings since Adam and Eve to exercise God-delegated dominion on the earth.

truth. No, according to Jesus, it was the humble. Fishermen, shopkeepers, day laborers, tax collectors, and sheep herders became the first human beings since Adam and Eve to exercise God-delegated dominion on the earth. This experience had been withheld from the proud and instead granted to those with childlike humility. *This* filled Jesus with hilarious joy.

But note also that Jesus cautioned the returning seventy about letting this privilege go to their heads. Immediately after confirming that He had indeed gifted His own authority to them (v. 19), again, Jesus said:

> "However, your real source of joy isn't merely that these spirits submit to your authority, but that your names are written in the journals of heaven and that you belong to God's kingdom. This is the true source of your authority." (v. 20 TPT)

This is a reminder to keep the main thing the main thing. Specifically, that the greatest source of excitement in our lives should always be that we belong to God and get to spend eternity discovering new wonders of His brilliance and love. It's also a reminder to rightly understand spiritual cause and effect. The gift of authority we've been given is an *effect* of being adopted by Him. The *cause* is the adoption. Keeping this in mind will keep us from taking pride in the authority and power we've received.

One of the New Testament's most widely known statements on pride connects humility with grace. James, quoting Psalm 34:8, writes,

> But He gives a greater grace. Therefore it says, "God is opposed to the proud, but gives grace to the humble." (James 4:6 NASB)

The contrast in this verse prompts me to think of grace as wind from heaven pushing and helping me forward toward the things God has called me to do. You don't have to be skilled in piloting sailboats to grasp that it's easier to sail to a destination with the wind behind you than to sail *into* the wind. Pride can cause the winds of heaven to turn around so that they actually create resistance to forward progress. Yes, many of God's people don't walk in the grace-gift of authority that belongs to them in Jesus simply because they're too prideful to receive it. But others let pride pull all of the heavenly wind out of their sails.

I must confess that I know what that feels like. On more than one occasion, I've let pride rob me of my capacity to walk in everything that ring of authority represents for me. I vividly recall one incident from my early days in ministry. I was young, zealous, and thrilled to have found a role traveling with a nationally known evangelist. I ministered in high schools and in youth rallies in advance of a coming evangelistic crusade. And I assisted in numerous ways during the large crusade events themselves. It was pretty heady stuff for a young man who really hadn't even been saved all that long.

On this particular night, during the altar call, a woman who had come forward started exhibiting signs of demonic influence. To keep her from becoming a distraction to those coming forward for salvation, she was taken to a private room in the back where she could receive ministry. Now, this book is not the place to go into a deep, biblical explanation of the reality of demonic influences on people. If you're unaware of these things, you'll just have to take my word for it that people, even Christians, experience varying degrees of demonic influence. And occasionally that influence grows to become what the Bible calls a stronghold. (All the more reason to understand our spiritual authority in Jesus!)

On this night, the evangelist, my employer and mentor, said to the staff members escorting the woman back to the room, "Go find Robert Morris and bring him back there. He can handle this situation." When they found me and told me, I immediately felt a surge of significance and importance well up inside me. I remember thinking, *Hey, I guess I'm the man! Apparently when you need a man of spiritual power, I'm now the guy they call on. Cool!* I recall thinking about the case reported in the seventeenth chapter of Matthew where the disciples repeatedly failed to cast some demons out of the young boy. Ultimately, they had to call Jesus in to get the job done. In my immature and insecure imagination, I'm Jesus in this scenario. The others couldn't get the job done in this difficult case, so they've called in "the big gun."

When I arrived in the room and walked through the door, I saw a tall woman sitting in a chair writhing as two large men struggled with all their strength to restrain her. Oh, and she was growling and snarling like a rabid wolf. I had just stepped into the room and taken in the startling scene when, with a single convulsion of her body, she violently threw both men holding on to her arms against the wall behind her. It was as if they were rag dolls. Then she looked right at me and hissed, "I've been waiting for you."

> In an instant, every drop of swagger, courage, and confidence I'd carried into that room drained out of me.

In an instant, every drop of swagger, courage, and confidence I'd carried into that room drained out of me. Fortunately, I'd been to the restroom recently, otherwise other things might have drained out of me, too. I was utterly paralyzed with fear and uncertainty. I honestly wanted to turn and run out of the room, but pride kept my feet anchored in place. So I just stood there frozen and speechless, with every eye in the room looking at me…"the man"!

Then, after what felt like an eternity, I heard a female voice from a corner of the room softly but firmly say two words.

"*Stop it.*"

I turned in the direction of the voice and saw a tiny elderly lady who couldn't have weighed more than ninety-five pounds. Her clothing and hair suggested she was neither sophisticated nor wealthy. She wasn't looking at me. The little grandma had locked eyes with the poor, tormented woman who had just violently tossed two grown men across the room. I hadn't even noticed her, but apparently she had been sitting over in the corner praying. I watched her rise, walk toward the woman, and point a bony, work-weathered finger in the woman's direction.

"Stop it," she repeated at a volume just loud enough to be heard by the woman and in a tone suggestive of the way a second-grade teacher would speak to a rambunctious, naughty boy. "You stop it right now. You hush and stop making a scene. And you let this precious woman go in the name of the Lord Jesus Christ, by the power of the Word of God, and by the blood of the Lamb."

Immediately the tormented woman collapsed in her chair as if utterly exhausted. The tiny grandma knelt down in front of her and took her face in her gnarled hands, brushed her hair out of her face, and said with profound kindness, "It's okay, sweetie, they're gone." And they were. The woman fell into the older woman's arms, sobbing in relief.

From that time forward, I've brought that incident to mind anytime I've been tempted to think I was God's man of power for the hour. I'll never forget that humble little grandmother who knew how to use the ring of authority she'd received as a gift from her Father. Yes, the first of three keys to walking in the grace-gift of authority is humility. God gives grace to the humble.

> I'll never forget that humble little grandmother who knew how to use the ring of authority she'd received as a gift from her Father.

The second of those keys is *faith*, or simply *belief*. Most believers have not even been told they have a ring of authority with Jesus' name on it. As a result, they have no faith for trampling on "serpents and scorpions." They have no faith for praying with power or speaking with authority so God's will is done as freely on earth as it is done in the realm of heaven. Faith is a big deal. Jesus talked about faith all the time. Praised it. Looked for it. Expressed dismay when it wasn't present. Seemed delighted when it was.

Do you recall what Jesus asked the disciples when they were on a boat on the sea of Galilee in the middle of a raging storm? After the panicking disciples had woken the sleeping Savior and he'd spoken three, one-syllable words to calm the storm ("Peace, be still"), Jesus turned to them and said, "Why are you so fearful? *How is it that you have no faith?*" (Mark 4:39–40, emphasis added). Here and on several other occasions, Jesus seems to be pointing out that the disciples were not exercising the authority He'd delegated to them because they didn't remember or believe they had it.

You see, it is one thing to possess authority. It is another thing to know it and wield it. One of the greatest illustrations of the link between faith and authority is found in the story of the Roman centurion in the eighth chapter of Matthew.

> Now when Jesus had entered Capernaum, a centurion came to Him, pleading with Him, saying, "Lord, my servant is lying at home paralyzed, dreadfully tormented." And Jesus said to him, "I will come and heal him." (Matthew 8:5–7)

Jesus was accustomed to encountering people who had faith to believe that if Jesus came and was physically present, He could miraculously heal. Remember how Jairus pleaded with Jesus to come to His house to heal his dying daughter (see Matthew 9:18–26)? Or how Mary and Martha sent word for Jesus to come quickly when their brother Lazarus fell deathly ill (John 11:3)? Such examples exhibit a level of faith, without a doubt. It was faith that miracles were possible *if* Jesus was physically present. Jesus initially assumed that this was the level of the centurion's faith as well, so He said, "I will come and heal him." But in response the centurion says something that causes Jesus to marvel.

> The centurion answered and said, "Lord, I am not worthy that You should come under my roof. But only speak a word, and my servant will be healed. *For I also am a man under authority, having soldiers under me. And I say to this one, 'Go,' and he goes; and to another, 'Come,' and he comes; and to my servant, 'Do this,' and he does it.*" (v. 8–9, emphasis added)

In the Roman military system, a centurion was the commanding officer of a "century" of soldiers, usually eighty soldiers plus support personnel. Six such centuries combined to make up a Roman *cohort* of around five hundred soldiers. And ten cohorts combined to create a Roman *legion* of roughly five thousand soldiers. Centurions were career military men, meaning they spent their entire lives in the army until either death in combat or old age retired them. So the man standing before Jesus had a deep, experiential understanding of delegated authority. He had men under him who unquestioningly obeyed his commands, even if it meant certain death. Yet he, too, was a man under authority. He unquestioningly obeyed the orders he received. He was accustomed to sending orders to remote locations and to receiving orders from remote locations.

Somehow, this Gentile perceived that Jesus wielded great authority in the same way. He assumed that, as a human, Jesus must be under authority, and He was! Jesus said He only did and said those things He saw His heavenly Father doing and saying. But the centurion also perceived that Jesus had tremendous authority. Which is why he said, "But only speak a word, and my servant will be healed" (v. 8). In other words, "You don't need to be physically present, Jesus. I know that all you have to do is just give the command."

Please note Jesus' response to the centurion's expression of faith in Jesus' authority:

When Jesus heard it, He marveled, and said to those who followed, "Assuredly, I say to you, I have not found such *great faith*, not even in Israel!" (v. 10, emphasis added)

The faith Jesus had encountered among His Jewish brothers and sisters was the kind that assumed Jesus needed to be physically present for His commands to have an effect. But this soldier had a clearer revelation of delegated authority. And that understanding produced in him, in Jesus' words, "great faith."

Clearly, faith is an important factor in determining the degree to which we operate in the authority we have been gifted in Jesus. This presents a question you may already be asking in your head: What undermines our faith, or confident belief, in the authority Jesus has delegated to us? Over the years I've learned that it's not always unbelief. Often, it's what I would call *mis-belief*. That is, believing something that isn't true. A blunt way to describe this is: "Believing a lie."

I'm reminded of a season of time several years ago in which it seemed the devil was attacking my wife cruelly and relentlessly. She came down with a terrible case of shingles. If you've never had shingles, those who have had it will testify that it can be one the most painful things they've ever experienced. The outbreak carried on week after week. Then, to add to her misery, she came down with a severe case of the flu. After several days of fever, chills, and body aches she saw a doctor.

Afterward we had a conversation in our kitchen. She reported that the doctor had said the flu symptoms usually lasted five to seven days. Previously, another doctor had told her that the shingles outbreak could last between four and eight weeks. So as we discussed all the medical reports, we noted that Debbie was on day four of the flu that the doctor has said would likely last five to seven days. So we figured, "Okay, day five is tomorrow. Let's hope for the low end of that range and pray that she'll feel better after tomorrow!" We used similar logic on the shingles, reasoning, "Okay, the doctor said four to eight weeks on the shingles, and this is week number four. So we can set our faith and hope in the low end of that range. Let's agree that this will be the last week of shingles."

After that conversation, I went out to the garage to putter around a bit. Five minutes later Debbie came through the door crying and holding a white kitchen towel around her hand. Then I watched the towel rapidly turn crimson right in front of my eyes. I quickly learned that she had been washing a large glass flower vase in our concrete sink. The soap-covered vase slipped from her hand and she reflexively went to catch it. Her hands were rapidly moving downward just as the vase was hitting the hard sink and shattering into jagged shards. Fingers and thumbs came down forcefully into the broken glass, ultimately requiring many stitches in the emergency room. It was our third trip to a medical facility in a thirty-day span.

I vividly recall having a specific thought as I was walking my bleeding wife through the doors of the ER. In my mind, I said, "Satan, why don't you fight like a man? If you want to fight, come after me. Quit coming after my wife, you miserable coward." It was anger and frustration speaking. That line of thinking wasn't particularly helpful from a spiritual standpoint, but the thought led me down a more constructive road, and ultimately opened a door for the Holy Spirit to speak to me. Sitting in the waiting room, I started wondering and asking the Lord, "Why am I not being able to cover Debbie? I'm her covering. Why am I seemingly not being able to protect her from all these attacks?" The cry of my heart was, "*Why?*"

> In that moment, I heard the familiar voice of the Spirit within me say, "It is because you've believed a lie."

In that moment, I heard the familiar voice of the Spirit within me say, "It is because you've believed a lie."

Keep in mind that faith, or *belief in the truth*, is a major key to exercising the authority we've been gifted by the Father in Jesus. And as I said previously, there is both unbelief and *mis-belief*. Unbelief is essentially doubting what God has said. But mis-belief is accepting something that isn't true—in other words, believing a lie. Another term for "believing a lie" is *deception*. Jesus once described Satan as the father of lies (see John 8:44).

In John 8:32 Jesus said the truth that we know, or the truth that is revealed to us, sets us free. The Greek word translated "truth" in Jesus' declaration is *aletheia*, and it means "reality, or what is really real." And there are always spiritual realities that we can't perceive with our senses, yet they are as much or more "real" than what our senses can perceive. Belief is so powerful! When we believe a lie, we're subject to a lack of freedom in that area. Another way to frame it is that we don't, in that area of deception, walk in the authority we've been gifted in Jesus, so we live in bondage. We're not "free" in that area.

In that moment of asking God for light and revelation about what was going on with my wife, I heard the Lord say, "In fact, you have believed two lies." That got my attention, so I pressed in for more insight.

"What lies have I believed?" I asked.

"When this wave of trouble started, you accepted it as *normal*."

I instantly recognized the truth of this. When Debbie got shingles we both sort of shrugged and essentially said, "This happens to people. We know a lot of people who have had shingles. This is a normal thing."

Then she got an infection that is very common. And again we figured, "This happens. It's a part of life." Then about the time that infection had run its course, she got the flu. And we said, "It's going around. This is normal."

I recognized the mis-belief that had subtly crept into our thinking as a couple. But then I remembered that the Spirit had mentioned *two* lies. So I pressed in for more light.

The Lord said, "It is normal and common for the enemy to war against My children, but it is *not* normal for My children to lose." Then the Spirit instantly brought several biblical examples to my remembrance.

"Yes, the Egyptian army pursued and cornered the Israelites, but that army drowned while my people walked away unscathed. Yes, Daniel got thrown into the lion's den, but I shut the mouths to the lions and Daniel walked away untouched. Yes, Shadrach, Meshach, and Abednego were thrown into a red-hot furnace, but they walked out not even smelling like smoke. Son, my Word reveals that it's normal to be attacked, but it's not normal to lose. You guys started believing it was normal to lose."

That stung. But it was true. Even after walking with God and pastoring a church for decades, I'm still learning. It's so important to believe the truth rather than lies. Which is why the ministry of the Holy Spirit is so vital in our lives. Why? Because Jesus told us that one of the Spirit's many wonderful roles is to "guide you into all truth" (John 16:13). In other words, to expose the areas in which you've been deceived. Areas in which you've believed a lie. Areas in which you have applied the power of faith to a falsehood.

Here's a question. In Ephesians Chapter 6, where we find the list of "the whole armor" of God, what piece of the armor is "able to quench all the fiery darts of the wicked one"? (v. 11, 16). The shield, of course! But the shield of what? Faith! Faith—believing the truth, embracing spiritual reality with all your heart and mind—quenches every flaming arrow of the enemy. Yes, we should expect some fights. But we should also expect to win because we have the Father's ring.

> Yes, we should expect some fights. But we should also expect to win because we have the Father's ring.

So far, we've identified two keys to effectively walk in the authority Jesus delegated to us—humility and faith. Here's the third.

Consecration. That's a fancy theological term that simply means "complete surrender to God's will and ways." In daily life, authentic consecration involves the habit of responding when the Holy Spirit nudges. "For as many as are led by the Spirit of God, these are sons of God," we're told in Romans 8:14. This is how sons and daughters of

> Responsiveness to the promptings and directives of the Spirit characterizes believers who wear the ring of authority effectively.

186

the King walk in authority. Responsiveness to the promptings and directives of the Spirit characterizes believers who wear the ring of authority effectively.

Here's the hard, plain truth. It's just difficult for stiff-necked, willful, rebellious children to walk in authority because being stiff-necked, willful, and rebellious invariably involves lacking the previous two characteristics—humility and faith. If I'm being rebellious, it is almost a certainty that I'm being prideful and have believed a lie. And as we've seen, when you're in that condition, you don't see the victory and results a wearer of Jesus' ring of authority should naturally see.

Earlier in this chapter when talking about humility we looked at James 4:6, which says, "God resists the proud but gives grace to the humble." Let's now look at the very next verse: "Therefore submit to God. Resist the devil and he will flee from you" (v. 7).

It's not an accident that this verse follows the one about humility. Note the word *therefore*, which connects the two biblical declarations. Humility and submission to God are very much connected. And as that verse suggests, *both* are connected to victory over the devil.

Here's great news. As with everything else about your life in God, grace is the answer. Being in God's presence softens your heart. Just using your confident access to the throne of grace to remain connected to Him transforms you into a child who loves to hear and respond to the voice of the Spirit. It's not something you work up through willpower and

> Just using your confident access to the throne of grace to remain connected to Him transforms you into a child who loves to hear and respond to the voice of the Spirit.

discipline. It's an organic, effortless outgrowth of just being with your Father.

We still have more to discover about the wonders of God's grace as revealed in the parable of the prodigal. There is still a third gift he received from his welcoming, rejoicing father that we haven't explored.

CHAPTER 19

YOUR SHOES

You may have noticed that in recent years we've seen an explosion of interest in collecting and trading basketball shoes and other forms of athletic footwear. "Sneakerheads," they're called, and the closet-filling collections of some of the most passionate collectors—many of them teenagers—can easily run into the tens of thousands of dollars in value. It seems people will spend a lot of money for a pair of shoes.

Back in 2021, a collector at an auction paid $1.5 million for a pair of 1984 Michael Jordan Nike Air Ships. Jordan himself wore this particular pair of shoes in his fifth professional basketball game in his rookie season. Back in 1989, jewelry designer Harry Winston created a pair of ruby slippers to commemorate the fiftieth anniversary of the debut of *The Wizard of Oz*. Whereas the shoes worn by Judy Garland in the 1939 movie were covered in cheap red sequins, Winston's re-creation was blanketed in real rubies. The shoes sold for more than $3 million. Other pairs of jewel-encrusted shoes have sold for upward of $17 million to wealthy Arab oil magnates. But historically shoes have been more of a practical necessity than a sign of status.

It seems that as long as there have been feet, thorns, and sharp rocks, people have been making and wearing shoes. In 1991, high in the Italian Alps, a thawing glacier revealed the frozen body of a man who died more than five thousand years ago. The perfectly preserved body of the man scientists named Ötzi was warmly dressed in clothing that included a pair of stitched leather boots. Ancient bodies of people pulled out of bogs in Scotland, recovered from the sands of the Sahara, and discovered in Egyptian tombs all sported shoes of some type.

The Bible contains many significant references to shoes, and if you examine all those references as a whole, you start to get the impression that shoes have symbolic meaning. Moses was instructed to remove his shoes before approaching God in the burning bush (see Exodus 3:5). Likewise, Joshua was instructed to remove his sandals in the presence of "the Commander of the LORD's army" (Joshua 5:15). By the way, based on other Scriptures, I believe that "Commander" was Jesus, the pre-incarnate Son of God. John the Baptist declared, concerning the Messiah, that He was not worthy to remove His sandals. Footwear is a prominent part of the "whole armor of God" (Ephesians 6:11, 15).

Then, of course, there is the verse we've been examining over the last few chapters:

> "But the father said to his servants, 'Bring out the best robe and put it on him, and put a ring on his hand and sandals on his feet.'" (Luke 15:22)

We've already explored the significance of the first two items the father of the prodigal gifted to his returning son—a robe and a ring. A search of Scripture revealed that both of those items carried profound meaning in its symbolic vocabulary. Shoes are no exception.

We're about to see that shoes represent *rights*. So it follows that the act of taking off shoes signifies the surrendering of rights. Do we see that anywhere in the Bible? Of course we do!

Now, if you have eyes to see it, everything in the Old Testament points to Jesus. That's why it's so important to read the Old Covenant through a New Covenant lens. Otherwise, you'll end up pulling pieces of Law forward that God never intended. You'll just get confused and double-minded. And as we saw in the chapter titled "A Better Husband," that's like trying to please your nitpicky ex-spouse while you're married to a wonderful, generous new spouse. Reading the old with a lens of the new means looking for Jesus. And one of the most beautiful and moving types and foreshadowings of what Jesus did for us is a love story found in the book of Ruth.

> Reading the old with a lens of the new means looking for Jesus.

I won't take the time to recount the whole story, especially because I suspect you're familiar with it. (If not, you can easily read Ruth's four chapters in one sitting.) In the consummation of the story, the widow Ruth is rescued and blessed and elevated to a much higher status by Boaz, a relative of her late husband. That rescue comes in the form of a relative's willingness to serve in a role called the kinsman redeemer. That role, and the ceremony that inaugurates it, was rooted in Levitical law and deep cultural traditions from that part of the world.

Ruth, having made a covenantal commitment to care for her mother-in-law, finds herself living in a strange land, destitute, and providing for the two of them by gleaning the fields of wealthy landowners. Levitical law required faithful Israelites to refrain from harvesting the grain from the corners of their fields. (Imagine a square field that you harvest in a circle.) That grain was to be left for the poor of the land. Greedy farmers who didn't care about God's instructions would routinely ignore this command. But once Boaz, a good, observant, and faithful man, discovered that the wife and daughter-in-law of his dead relative were dependent on unharvested grain for survival, he ordered his field hands to leave extra grain unharvested.

Because women could not inherit in ancient Israel, the kinsman-redeemer rite was established to restore ancestral lands to widows through remarriage. Ordinarily the responsibility to redeem belonged to the nearest male relative. You may recall an incident in which a gaggle of Sadducees tried to trip Jesus up with a hypothetical question about a woman whose husband dies, and his oldest brother marries her in accordance with the Law. Then that guy dies, so the next brother steps up. He dies, and the process repeats until the poor woman has gone through all the brothers of her original husband (see Matthew 22:23–32).

Boaz loved Ruth and wanted to marry her in fulfillment of this process, even though the process required purchasing—that is, "redeeming"—the lands that originally belonged to Ruth's late husband and her mother-in-law's late husband. But Boaz wasn't first in line. Another relative of Ruth's late husband stood ahead of him. So Boaz went to him to see if he was prepared to fulfill the role of the kinsman redeemer. To Boaz's relief and delight, the guy essentially said, "I'll pass," even though it was technically his responsibility according to the Law. He likely passed because it was expensive, and it meant taking on more responsibility—not just a wife but her mother-in-law as well. That left the way clear for Boaz who, out of a heart of love, was more than happy to part with the money and take on the responsibility. Assuming that covenantal responsibility was consummated in a ceremony.

Even today, we have long-standing traditions concerning another covenantal ceremony—the wedding. The walking down the aisle by the father, the exchange of rings, the kiss, and the throwing of the bride's bouquet are all examples. In a similar way, stepping in as the kinsman redeemer involved a ceremony. We find one very ancient, very specific element of that ritual in this verse:

> Now this was the custom in former times in Israel concerning redeeming and exchanging, to confirm anything: *one man took off his sandal and gave it to the other*, and this was a confirmation in Israel. (Ruth 4:7, emphasis added)

Notice this verse says the removal and giving of a sandal is a sign in Israel to "confirm *anything*." Today we use pens to put ink signatures on contracts. Here, the public giving of a shoe signifies the surrendering of a right—in this case, the right to be the kinsman redeemer. It is a surrender of the right to take Ruth as a wife and to purchase the ancestral, tribal lands belonging to her late husband. The removal of the shoe, or shoes, was a legally binding way of signing away his rights.

With that truth in mind, let me point you back to a couple of examples I briefly cited a little earlier. I'm referring to the two separate times Moses and Joshua were commanded to remove their shoes as they stepped onto holy ground to speak directly with the Father and the Son. Doesn't this truth add an additional dimension of understanding to that act? As God began to reveal Himself to these men, he began by teaching them that it's always vital to approach with a posture of surrendered rights . . . that is, consecration.

Read that account in Joshua Chapter 5 of Joshua's encounter with the Commander of the Lord's armies and you'll see Joshua asking this question: "Are You for us or for our adversaries?" (v. 13). I can't help but laugh whenever I read the Lord's blunt, one-word reply to that question:

"No."

Ordinarily, "Are you for us or for our enemies" is not a yes-or-no question. But Jesus' reply is basically, "None of the above, Joshua. I'm not here to take sides. I'm here to take over." Put another way, when you're talking to Jesus, the question isn't whether or not He's for you. The question is, "Are you for Him?"

> When you're talking to Jesus, the question isn't whether or not He's for you. The question is, "Are you for Him?"

"Is He Lord?"

"Have you taken your shoes off?"

We saw in the previous chapter that one of the most common ways we negate our ability to walk in our God-given authority—symbolized by the ring—is to not live in consecration to God's will and ways. We can now see that in these two cases, the command to "remove your shoes" is a directive to be submitted to God's will and ways. It's no coincidence that both of these encounters involved God communicating *what* He wanted these men to do and *how* He wanted them to do it.

His will. His ways.

Here's the thing. As we saw early on in this journey, the very nature of the Old Covenant made people *servants* (or vassals). But the New Covenant makes them *sons*. (Please recall, I'm using the terms *sons* and *sonship* in a generic sense to refer to both sons and daughters of God.) In the Old Testament era, being a servant of God was a wonderful opportunity. It was, by far, the best deal in town. God's invitation to covenant connection was especially good because you were entering into a suzerain-vassal arrangement with a suzerain who was kind, generous, faithful, and merciful. But it's still better to be a son than a servant.

> The very nature of the Old Covenant made people *servants* (or vassals). But the New Covenant makes them *sons*.

We'll explore that further in the next chapter, but for now, turning your thoughts back to the parable of the prodigal, here's a question. If taking off your shoes means giving up your rights, what did it mean for the father to call for shoes to be placed on his son's feet?

The shoes here represent the complete and comprehensive restoration to the rights of sonship. As with every other grace-gift, the rights of sonship aren't earned. They aren't awarded. They come as a birthright.

> As with every other grace-gift, the rights of sonship aren't earned. They aren't awarded. They come as a birthright.

Now the picture may be coming together for you. We take our shoes off when we come to Jesus for salvation, surrendering our right to live our lives in our own strength and to make our own way in this broken world. And in response, the Father puts a new pair on us as a free gift. They are shoes of sonship.

Nevertheless, just as with the ring of authority, it's very possible to receive the shoes of sonship without experiencing all the benefits, blessings, and fruitfulness they convey. Those shoes are better than all the Air Jordans and ruby slippers in the world put together. So just ahead, we'll explore how to wear your amazing new shoes.

CHAPTER 20

WALKING IN YOUR RIGHTS AS SONS AND DAUGHTERS

I am very aware that not everyone had the blessing that I did of being born into a home with two great parents who loved and cared for me. But no matter what your situation was, you didn't earn, merit, or deserve your place at the table. My friends who were adopted didn't earn their place at the table in their adoptive homes, either. Your rights of sonship were not based on what you did, how smart you were, or how talented you were. No, those rights and privileges came simply by virtue of being a son or daughter. The same is true of you where your standing with your heavenly Father is concerned.

When you came to God through Jesus, God not only put a robe of Jesus' own righteousness around you, and a ring of Jesus' own delegated authority on your finger...but also placed the shoes of sonship on your feet! The rights that are yours as a child of God are stunning. But so few of God's children ever exercise them fully or consistently.

> Oh, what a privilege this becomes when the very God who spoke the universe into existence makes you His child and writes His own family name upon you.

What are those rights?

Well, first and foremost, every son or daughter receives the right to carry their father's name. Oh, what a privilege this becomes when the very God who spoke the universe into existence makes you His child and writes His own family name upon you. You're no doubt familiar with 2 Chronicles 7:14, which begins, "If my people who are called *by my Name*..." And because the Father and Son are one...we get Jesus' name as well.

This is something orphans long for. We don't have many true orphanages in this country anymore, but there was a time when they were commonplace. Today there are so many couples and families who would love to adopt a child that agencies search the globe to find one for them, at great cost. But wherever there are older orphans, you'll find children who would give anything to have a kind father come and say, "You're one of mine now. You're in my family and you will have my name from now on."

Here's another right that comes with those shoes. Sons and daughters have *access* to the father that servants simply don't enjoy.

When I was growing up, my father owned a successful company. He employed quite a few people relative to the size of our little town and owned two multistory buildings in the heart of it. As a kid, I loved it when I got to go up and see my dad at work. I recall standing in front of one of those buildings that seemed so huge to me as a kid and, at the top of that building, seeing my name in big letters. MORRIS.

It made me feel important. That was *my* name! Of course, I'd had nothing at all to do with why those particular letters were there. It was my father's years of hard work, frugality, good stewardship, and wisdom—being a man God could bless—that put that Morris name on those structures. But that didn't stop young me from feeling like a big deal.

When I got old enough to drive and work a part-time job, he took me on as an entry-level employee. And when I went off to college, I'd still work for him when I came home for the summer. I vividly remember an incident that occurred on my first day back after my freshman year in college. I and several of the other grunt-work guys were sitting in a trailer out on a job site receiving our assignments from a relatively new supervisor. That foreman had no idea who I was. To him I was just another shaggy-haired college kid working a summer job.

He had just gotten started when we all saw my father's car pull up. The man got a smug frown on his face and said, "Oh, here comes Mr. Big." Please keep in mind, at this point in my life I'm an unsaved, smart-mouthed kid with a whole year of college under my belt. So I decided to have a little fun with this guy. I innocently asked, "Who's Mr. Big?"

He said, with a hint of derision in his voice, "That's J. P. Morris. He owns the company, and he thinks he runs things. But the truth is, *I'm* really the one who runs things around here." I smiled and nodded just as my father opened the door and said, "Hey everyone." Then he looked at Mr. Supervisor and said, "Is everything good? You need anything?" The man shook his head. Then my father looked at me and said, "Hey, son, welcome home. Since you just got back, do you want to grab lunch today?" I smiled and said, "Sure, Dad!"

Have you ever seen all the color drain out of a person's face? I did that day. I enjoyed that moment a little too much. But I remember thinking, *You may call him Mr. Big, but I call him Dad.* That's true of you concerning the God of the universe. Others may call Him God, Supreme Deity, Almighty, Providence, Creator of Heaven and Earth—and all of these title-names are appropriate. Yet you and I have been invited to call Him Father, Papa, Daddy:

> And you did not receive the "spirit of religious duty," leading you back into the fear of never being good enough. But you have received the "Spirit of full acceptance," enfolding you into the family of God. And you will never feel orphaned, for as he rises up within us, our spirits join him in saying the words of tender affection, "Beloved Father!" For the Holy Spirit makes God's fatherhood real to us as he whispers into our innermost being, "You are God's beloved child!" (Romans 8:15–16 TPT)

I remember another occasion a few years later. I had recently married Debbie and had gone back to work for my father. I had gotten myself into some sort of pickle or jam, which wasn't unusual back then, and I needed his help. So I drove up to his building, headed toward his office, walked past the handful of people waiting to meet with him and his "gatekeeper" assistant, and walked straight into his office.

No one else in that building could do that. But I could. Why? What gave me that confident access?

Sonship.

Once inside, I said, "Dad, I have a problem."

Immediately, my father stuck his head out of his office and said to his assistant, "Hold my calls and appointments for a bit, please. My son is here."

This is our spiritual reality. Sure, both sons and servants work and are productive in the "company." But only sons and daughters enjoy the right of free access to the father.

> For through Him [Jesus] we both have access by one Spirit to the Father. (Ephesians 2:18, addition mine)
>
> ...in whom [Jesus] we have boldness and access with confidence through faith in Him. (Ephesians 3:12, addition mine)
>
> Let us therefore come boldly to the throne of grace, that we may obtain mercy and find grace to help in time of need. (Hebrews 4:16)
>
> Therefore, brethren, having boldness to enter the Holiest by the blood of Jesus, by a new and living way which He consecrated for us, through the veil, that is, His flesh, and having a High Priest over the house of God, let us draw near with a true heart in full assurance of faith... (Hebrews 10:19–22a)

On most days, to outsiders, I might have looked like any other employee of J. P. Morris. But I had something only sons and daughters have. Access. It's one of the rights that come with the gift of those shoes.

There are many others. As with the symbol of the ring, the gift of the shoes of sonship confers a right to authority and power. As we saw in the previous chapter, a key part of that ring of authority we receive when we come to the Father through the Son is the delegated power to "trample on serpents and scorpions, and over

As with the symbol of the ring, the gift of the shoes of sonship confers a right to authority and power.

all the power of the enemy" (Luke 10:19). Well, with what part of your body do you "trample" on things? Your feet!

One of the most frequently repeated and referenced Old Testament Scriptures in the New Testament is Psalm 110:1. It's a Psalm of David, but he is prophetically hearing God say to Jesus, "Sit at My right hand, till I make Your enemies Your footstool." The writer of Hebrews referenced this verse when he wrote:

But this Man [Jesus], after He had offered one sacrifice for sins forever, sat down at the right hand of God, from that time waiting till His enemies are made His footstool. (Hebrews 10:12–13, addition mine)

Here's my question to you. Who are Jesus' hands and feet in this world? Who constitutes His body? You and I, of course! The Church is the body of Christ. We are to walk in the authority over Jesus' enemies—putting them under our feet—to such a degree that they, in a sense, become his footstool. But please keep in mind, our enemies are not people. God loves people so much that while we were still sinners Christ died for us (see Romans 5:8). No, Paul makes it clear who our (and Jesus') enemies are:

For we do not wrestle against flesh and blood, but against principalities, against powers, against the rulers of the darkness of this age, against spiritual hosts of wickedness in the heavenly places. (Ephesians 6:12)

Yes, the shoes represent our family right to authority and victory. But the shoes also confer the power to share the gospel and thereby expand God's family on the earth. Shoes are mentioned as "the preparation of the gospel of peace" in Paul's list of the "whole armor of God" in the sixth chapter of Ephesians (v. 11, 15). And Jesus told His disciples they would receive supernatural power to be His witnesses after the Holy Spirit fell upon them (see Acts 1:8–9).

Shoes also symbolize the right to freedom. We see this over in 2 Chronicles Chapter 28. There, a group of people from the southern kingdom, Judah, had been taken captive by a group from the northern kingdom, Israel. The first thing the captors did was take away the shoes of their captives. Why, in practical terms, would you take away the shoes of your prisoners? Because without shoes they couldn't run away. But soon a prophet appeared and told those who had taken the prisoners that if they didn't release them, God's judgment would fall on them. In response, they restored the captives' shoes and released them. Shoes mean freedom!

> Shoes also symbolize the right to freedom.

The shoes of sonship you received represent freedom from captivity and bondage to you, too. "It is for freedom that Christ has set us free" (Galatians 5:1a NIV). Across more than four decades in ministry, I've seen there are basically two areas in which God's sons and daughters end up in bondage or captivity. These are two areas in which believers unnecessarily surrender the freedom that comes with the shoes of sonship.

First, some go back into bondage to sin. Occasional unrighteous acts become habits. Habits progressively become strongholds. At some point, born-again children of God can find themselves in some sort of demonic prison in one or more areas of their lives. This doesn't mean they're not going to heaven. But it does mean they're not living in the freedom Jesus died to make possible for them. They're not walking in the shoes of sonship. To use Paul's metaphor from Romans Chapter 6, they've submitted themselves as "slaves to sin" rather than "slaves to righteousness" (v. 17–18).

There is a second area in which we can surrender our freedom. Many voluntarily go back into servitude to the Law. As we explored in the chapter titled "A Better Husband," they think and live as if they're still in a marriage to that former nitpicky, perfectionist, fault-finding, condemnation-dispensing husband, rather than in a marriage to Jesus who wrapped them in a robe of His own righteousness as an unmerited, unearned, undeserved gift. Paul wrote the entire book of Galatians to people who were in the process of doing that. It is there, right after declaring "it was for freedom that Christ has set us free...," that Paul pleads:

> Stand firm, then, and do not let yourselves be burdened again by *a yoke of slavery.* (Galatians 5:1b, emphasis added)

Notice the phrase *let yourselves* in that sentence. It's possible to allow yourself to gradually, bit by bit, step by step, move out of the Father's house and to make the bunkhouse—the servants' quarters—your primary residence.

In the previous chapter of Galatians, Paul makes this case using Abraham's two sons as a metaphor for living under Old Covenant Law

204

rather than under New Covenant grace. You may recall that after getting impatient and frustrated waiting for God to fulfill His promise to give Abraham and Sarah a child in their old age, the couple decided they would "help God" through their own natural efforts. Their idea was to have Abraham father a child through Sarah's servant Hagar. Thus Ishmael was born. Later, Sarah miraculously conceived with Abraham, which produced their son Isaac. Two sons with two different mothers. One was born from a slave through natural effort and ability. The other was born to a free woman through God's power and faith in His promise. Now note how Paul uses these events to describe two ways to live:

> Tell me, you who desire to be under the law, do you not listen to the law? For it is written that Abraham had two sons, one by a slave woman and one by a free woman. But the son of the slave was born according to the flesh, while the son of the free woman was born through promise. Now this may be interpreted allegorically: *these women are two covenants.* One is from Mount Sinai, bearing children for slavery; she is Hagar. Now Hagar is Mount Sinai in Arabia; she corresponds to the present Jerusalem, for she is in slavery with her children. But the Jerusalem above is free, and *she is our mother.* (Galatians 4:21–26 ESV, emphasis added)

Now imagine Paul telling a first-century Jewish person that the Mosaic Law is represented by Hagar and Ishmael, rather than Sarah and Isaac! Perhaps that sheds some light on why Paul was nearly beaten to death numerous times after preaching in a synagogue. Here Paul is telling people who are being persuaded to follow pieces of the Law, such as circumcision, that they've forgotten who their mother is. We are not children of the slave woman. We are born of the free woman. Again, it was for freedom that Christ set you free. Free from slavery to sin. Free from slavery to the Law. Free from oppression. Free from condemnation. Free from shame. This is the gift of sonship. Those shoes are pretty significant, don't you think? In fact, the spiritual meaning of all three gifts given to the Prodigal in Jesus' parable carry enormous significance for you and me as we live our daily lives.

But there was another son in that parable, wasn't there? Does he have some important things to teach us? You'd better believe it.

CHAPTER 21

SONS AND DAUGHTERS NOT SERVANTS

When Jesus delivered a parable, every word was significant. Our Savior was never careless with His words. Not only did He choose them with intentionality, but they came by inspiration of the Spirit. So we can safely assume there are no throwaway details in the parable of the prodigal son. One big detail comes toward the end of the story. There we learn more about the older brother. We briefly examined this brother's reaction to his Father's mercy, kindness, and love back in chapter 15. There I noted that Jesus initially told the parable in response to complaints and criticisms from the Pharisees about Jesus' willingness to engage with "tax collectors and sinners."

Our English word *parable* is built from two Greek words. The first is *para*, which means "separate from, yet alongside or beside." Thus, a *para*military group is an army that is separate from the nation's regular army but can fight alongside it. A *para*church ministry is a Christian organization that isn't a church, yet works alongside churches in doing the work of the kingdom.

The back half of the word *parable* is rooted in the Greek word *bolee*, which means "to throw or cast." In fact, in some Greek-speaking cultures, *bolee* came to be used as a rough unit of measurement, denoting the distance the average man could throw a stone. As in:

"Pardon me sir, I'm looking for the home of Demetrius Konstapopadopolis. Can you direct me?"

"Sure, walk about three *bolees* that way, take a right at the goat with a black patch in the shape of a fish on its side, and you'll find it four *bolees* down on the left."

So when you combine *para* and *bolee* into *parable*, you get a word that means "a story that is thrown out alongside a person or people to illustrate a truth." The truth is laid alongside a misconception or lie so it's easy to see the contrast—much in the same way laying a straight stick alongside a bent one makes it obvious that the crooked one isn't straight.

In this case, the scribes and Pharisees had bought into the crooked lie that God was looking for performance rather than relationship, and that a key part of that performance involved shunning people that God loved and wanted to reconnect with. So Jesus "threw out" a story about a father with two sons and "laid it alongside" that lie. In doing so, He exposed the assumptions of the scribes and Pharisees as being totally out of alignment with God's heart, values, and plans.

As you now know, those religious elitists were represented by the older brother in that parable. I suspect you're also starting to understand that we believers face a constant pull to become that older brother, too. That brother was a true, beloved son but lived and thought like a servant. He was earn-and-deserve-minded rather than graced-with-sonship-minded. The same is true for countless believers.

It's possible to receive the robe of righteousness, the ring of authority, and the shoes of sonship and then go back to living like a servant. And servants live in fear. Which is precisely why Paul uses the word *again* in the following verse:

> For you did not receive the spirit of bondage *again* to fear, but you received the Spirit of adoption by whom we cry out, "Abba, Father." The Spirit Himself bears witness with our spirit that we are children of God. (Romans 8:15–16, emphasis added)

Why "again?" Because we were at one time living in the bondage of fear and shame as long as we were married to the Law and slaves to sin. But that all changed when we died to the Law and were wed to Christ. We died and were *reborn*. And every new baby quickly learns to recognize the face of their father (*abba*). To go back to living the old way, in any sense, would be receiving again a spirit of bondage, leading to a life filled with fear.

We *come* to Jesus as the prodigal in the story, yet it's possible to *live* in Jesus as the older brother. And what a tragedy this is. As South African teacher John Sheasby writes in his book *The Birthright: Out of the Servants' Quarters into the Father's House*:

It is mindboggling to imagine how much the older brother forfeited as a result of his servant mentality. Think of all the times he could have taken a calf from his daddy's herd and had the servants prepare a feast for him and his friends. Think of the joy he could have experienced in drawing close to his daddy, working with him, talking with him, eating with him. Think of the love, the favor, the generosity he could have enjoyed.

These were all the son's rights by birth.[5]

The older brother missed out on all the joys of sonship, even though he was, in every conceivable way, a son. The same is possible for you and me. We can be sons and daughters and yet think and live like servants. Remember, sons work on the ranch, too. It's not like they spend their days in a hammock drinking lemonade. They are about their father's business. But they enjoy access and authority and blessings that servants don't. They eat at the father's table. They live in the father's house. In other words, they *serve*, but they're not *servants*.

Here's another thing Jesus shows us about the servant mindset. The older brother deeply resented the way the father restored all the blessings of sonship to his wayward brother. When he got the word concerning the return of his brother, and of the father's plans for a celebration, Jesus says:

> "But he was angry and would not go in. Therefore his father came out and pleaded with him. So he answered and said to his father, 'Lo, these many years *I have been serving you; I never transgressed your commandment at any time*; and yet you never gave me a young goat, that I might make merry with

my friends. But as soon as this son of yours came, who has devoured your livelihood with harlots, you killed the fatted calf for him.'" (Luke 15:28–30, emphasis added)

Note that this brother defines his status with his father on the basis of his performance rather than their relationship. He says, "I have been serving you" and "I never transgressed your commandment at any time." We apparently have a miracle here. We've found the first perfect child in recorded history! I joke, yet this is a danger for us, as well. The moment we start defining ourselves—our lives in God—in terms of what we do and don't do, we've lost the plot. It is not that our actions are irrelevant. It's not that our mistakes don't damage ourselves and others. It's that our standing with the Father isn't built on *our* righteousness. It's built on Jesus' righteousness and on the fact that, through Him, we have been "born of God" (1 John 5:4). We're not His because of our *service*. We're His because we're His *seed*. The moment we forget that... the moment we define our connection and rights in terms of how well we behave and how hard we serve... the next inevitable step is to start resenting our siblings who live as if they're free.

> It's not that our mistakes don't damage ourselves and others. It's that our standing with the Father isn't built on *our* righteousness.

There is another term that aptly describes the mistaken postures and beliefs of both the prodigal and his older brother: *orphan spirit*. That's a term that many insightful Christian teachers and writers have used over the years to describe a failure to understand every believer's adopted sonship with the Father. Just above we revisited the passage in Romans Chapter 8 in which Paul talks about the "spirit of adoption" (v. 15) that God gives us the moment we're born again. One that, if we have a heart to hear, cries out "Abba!" (daddy, dear poppa) to the God of the universe. But many believers, and I was one of them, were essentially taught from the moment we were born again to ignore that heart cry. To use a different metaphor, we are all born again at the Tree of Life, but almost immediately, well-intentioned people took us by the hand and led us over to the Tree of the Knowledge of Good and Evil. There, we were taught to read the Bible like a rule book rather than as a living, active revelation of God's Father-heart.

The orphan lives insecure concerning his standing in the house and therefore constantly works and strives to earn his place at the table. The orphan is fear-driven and endlessly haunted by her sense of dis-connection and dis-relation to the father. The orphan spirit is Adam and Eve, cowering in the shadows in shame and fear, even while a loving Creator is searching for them.

> The orphan lives insecure concerning his standing in the house and therefore constantly works and strives to earn his place at the table.

In his excellent book *Orphans No More: Learning to Live Loved*, Dudley Hall writes:

> The greatest invitation ever offered comes from the Father to the orphaned sons of Adam. Through the life, death, resurrection, and ascension of Jesus the Son, we can be restored to the original design... From the cross He declared the anguished cry of the orphan, "My God... why have you forsaken me." He became the orphan so we could become the sons of God. Now we no longer have to strive to get back to

the Father. There is no price to pay or regulations to keep that will qualify us. We are declared, "sons of God" by none other than the Father Himself.[6]

Is it possible that we've been so fixated on not becoming the prodigal—rebellious, sinful, and out of control—that we've allowed ourselves to become the older brother? I suspect many have. Joyless. Lonely. Prideful. Obsessively comparing ourselves with others to see if we're doing better than they are. And exhausted from a constant striving to earn and merit as a servant when everything already belongs to us as sons.

Please recall that in Jesus' parable, the father divided his entire estate to *both* brothers (see Luke 15:12). From the moment the younger brother took off to do his own thing, out from under the shelter of the father's protective covering, the rest of the estate legally belonged to the older brother. That means he lied when he angrily said to his father:

> "Lo, these many years I have been serving you; I never transgressed your commandment at any time; *and yet you never gave me a young goat*, that I might make merry with my friends." (Luke 15:29, emphasis added)

The resentful young man could have taken a goat or a calf or any other asset on the ranch and used it in any way he pleased at any time. Take that in for a moment. He's accusing his father of not being generous, when the dad had already given him everything! The moment the father divided his estate between his two sons, the elder son was legally a co-owner with the father. So why was he so miserable and disappointed and frustrated and resentful? Because he was legally a son, but he had the mindset of a servant.

He thought of his father as a suzerain and of himself as a vassal—working his tail off desperately hoping to be rewarded with some recognition and some scraps from the owner's table. When all along a place at the table and access to everything on it belonged to him.

But don't be too quick to judge him harshly. How often have we done precisely the same thing with the God who pursued us, chose us, adopted us, and made us His own? How often have we treated him like a harsh suzerain rather than a loving father? How often have we struggled, strained, strived, flailed, and floundered trying to earn something that was already legally ours? How often have we quietly—in our deepest heart of hearts—resented God for withholding good things from us?

Let's examine the patient father's reply to his son's angry outburst. There's gold in it for you:

> "And he said to him, 'Son, you are always with me, and all that I have is yours. It was right that we should make merry and be glad, for your brother was dead and is alive again, and was lost and is found.'" (Luke 15:31–32)

Jesus puts three extraordinary points into the mouth of the father here. Again, Jesus knew what He was talking about. Every word of this parable is filled with significance. First the father says, "Son, you are always with me."

Son . . . The Greek word used here is *teknon*. In many other places in the New Testament a different Greek word for "son," *huios*, is used. *Huios* is a gender-specific word that means male descendant, whether young or an adult. But *teknon* isn't gender-specific. It refers to a child—male or female—who is dependent on a parent. It connotes a child who is deeply cherished.

We may, from time to time, think we're disqualified as children of the Father. That we've done too much wrong or fallen too far short for the joys and privileges of sonship. That servant status is what we deserve and is the best that we can hope for. But God never thinks that. The returning prodigal thought he had forfeited his sonship rights and blessings, but the moment he returned, the father did all he could do to show that wasn't true. And here the resentful brother with a hired hand's mindset is instantly reminded of the truth in a single word. *Son.*

What follows that affectionate reaffirmation of identity is a reminder of the greatest sonship blessing of all. This patient, gracious father had to point out to this knothead that he possessed a treasure far beyond some fatted calf, or even all the cattle and land on the ranch. And he'd had this treasure all along! The father said, "You are always with *me*."

As a son rather than a servant, he had the privilege of unrestricted access to the father. His father's wisdom and counsel were always available to him. But more important, in contrast with every servant on the ranch, he could simply enjoy being *with* his wonderful dad. To eat with him. Sit by a fire with him and look in wonder at the stars on a crystal-clear night. To work beside him, learning how and why he did things a certain way. He was afforded a privilege every employee on the ranch would have given

> If you've been born of God through the miracle of the new birth, you are a *teknon*—the cherished child of a gracious, generous Father.

anything to enjoy. But this young man instead had either taken this for granted or, even worse, neglected the privilege because he had the mindset of a hired hand.

So what about you? If you've been born of God through the miracle of the new birth, you are a *teknon*—the cherished child of a gracious, generous Father. And the first message for you in the Father's response is "Child, you are always with me." With the same boldness displayed by my teenage self—who once barged into my father's business office without an appointment—the way to the Father's presence is always wide open for you. Jesus is that "way." In fact, in Hebrews 10:20 the New King James calls Him a "new and living way" into the Father's most intimate presence. Look at that passage in context in The Passion Translation:

And now we are brothers and sisters *in God's family* because of the blood of Jesus, and he welcomes us to come into the most holy sanctuary in the heavenly realm—*boldly and without hesitation.* For he has dedicated a new, life-giving way for us to approach God. For just as the veil was torn in two, Jesus' body was torn open to give us free and fresh access to him!

And since we now have a magnificent High Priest to welcome us into God's house, we come closer to God and *approach him with an open heart, fully convinced that nothing will keep us at a distance from him.* For our hearts have been sprinkled with blood to remove impurity, and we have been freed from an accusing conscience. Now we are clean, unstained, and presentable to God inside and out! (Hebrews 10:19–22, emphasis added)

This is: Grace, Period.

It is the magnificent grace of God displayed through the complete and finished work of His only begotten son, Jesus. The first and greatest unearned, undeserved, unmerited gift we receive as sons and daughters is this complete cleansing that—if we understand it, believe it, and root it into our identities—gives us the confidence to run to our Father "boldly and without hesitation." To just be *with* Him throughout our days. To commune with Him. To learn His ways. To discover the inexhaustible wonders of His heart.

But there is more. Jesus has the father in His parable cite a second blessing of sonship: "All that I have is yours."

Again, the father in the parable—contrary to all convention and tradition—willingly divided his estate to his two sons while he was still living. When he said, "All that I have is yours," he was stating a legal fact. You may recall how, in one of the earlier chapters in this book, we explored the difference between a suzerain-vassal covenant and a parity covenant, the latter being a sacred agreement between two peers or equals. We observed that the Mosaic Covenant was patterned after that first kind, but that the New Covenant is built upon a covenantal agreement between God the Father and God the Son who willingly became one of us so He could serve as a proxy, or stand-in, for us in that arrangement.

Additionally, we saw that in a parity covenant, each party pledges to the other access to all of their resources. Another way of saying this would be exactly what the father in the parable said: "All that I have is yours." Because the miraculous new birth puts us legally and spiritually in Christ, what God the Father says to His covenant partner, He is also saying to us.

This is the legal and spiritual foundation of the mind-blowing

statements in the Gospel of John that Jesus makes to all those who
follow him:

> And whatever you ask in My name, that I will do, that the
> Father may be glorified in the Son. (John 14:13)
> If you abide in Me, and My words abide in you, you will
> ask what you desire, and it shall be done for you. (John 15:7)
> All things that the Father has are Mine. Therefore I said
> that He [the Spirit] will take of Mine and declare it to you.
> (John 16:15, addition mine)

One of the most prominent and defining characteristics of our
heavenly Father is His generosity. The entirety of Scripture testifies
to this. Of course, children natu-
rally take after their fathers. Which
is why I frequently point out that we
are never more like our Father than
when we are being generous. Live
in God's presence like a true son or
daughter for a while and you'll discover this. And once you discover it,
you'll find yourself free to be generous, too.

> One of the
> most prominent
> and defining
> characteristics of
> our heavenly Father
> is His generosity.

People with the mindset of a hired hand—people like the older
son in Jesus' parable—never feel free to be generous because they
have a scarcity mindset. They never know if they've earned enough
heavenly credits to get their needs met. They don't see God as a
Father who has looked at them and declared, "All I have is yours."

Kris Vallaton of Bethel Church in Redding, California, tells a
stunning story of fostering a boy, Eddie, who had lived his whole
life in the care of a drug-addicted mother.[7] The boy had practically

raised himself. The basics such as food and electricity had been sporadic and unpredictable his entire life. When Kris and his wife were granted custody of Eddie, they instantly noticed something at mealtime. Even though the table was invariably heaped with food, the boy watched the serving bowls like a hawk. When one of the bowls reached the half-full point, he would quickly refill his plate. When he thought no one was looking, he would stash food in his napkin and carry it into his bedroom. Life as a near orphan had marked the boy's young soul with a scarcity mindset.

Eventually Eddie came to understand that there was always going to be plenty of food. That even when the table was nearly empty, there was more where that came from. He learned that there were stores of food and access to food that he couldn't even imagine. Only then did he begin to relax and stop hoarding. Only then could he be liberated from his prison of scarcity thinking and scarcity behaving.

The same is true for all former orphans like you and me. We can carry a scarcity mindset into our new adoptive home. But the reality of having a forever-place at God's heavenly banquet table is that everything we could ever need for life and godliness—that is, physical needs and spiritual needs—has been fully, infinitely supplied because we're in Jesus (see 2 Peter 1:3). Yet if we're still carrying around the orphan/servant/vassal/older-brother identity, our impulse will be to hoard rather than to give. We will wrongly view our Father as hard and tight-fisted. And so instead of holding everything God has given us with an open hand, we will be tight-fisted, too.

In his devotional titled *Praying Grace*, my friend David Holland included this prayer of repentance at the end of one of the devotions.

Wonderful Father, forgive me for any time I have approached You as if You were anything less than extravagantly generous. Or if my heart has ever seemed to question Your goodness. Your gift of Jesus shouts of Your love and compassion toward me. What a gift! And when I see what He suffered on my behalf, I stand in awe of Your grace.

I will not insult Your extravagant love by coming to You as a beggar—or as if I need to find some way to overcome Your reluctance to supply my needs and bless. You are generous. You, dear Father, did not spare Your own Son, but gave Him up for me. How will You not also, along with him, graciously meet my every need.[8]

> For the child of God, scarcity is a lie. Yet so many of God's people have a scarcity mindset.

For the child of God, scarcity is a lie. Yet so many of God's people have a scarcity mindset. They believe provision is scarce and so they hoard. They believe that love is scarce, so they become needy, clingy, and insecure. They believe that significance is scarce, so they inwardly resent it when one of their siblings receives recognition or promotion or blessing. Which leads us to the third item in the father's response to his angry, resentful eldest son.

Recall that the father said, "It was right that we should make merry and be glad, for your brother was dead and is alive again, and was lost and is found." A hired-hand mentality will keep you constantly comparing yourself with others. Relentlessly looking around at your siblings to see who seems to have more than you. It often manifests as arrogance, boastfulness, and pride, but the root is the orphan's insecurity. Only those secure in their identities as beloved *teknons* are free to celebrate the successes and blessings of others. Only the secure will hold everything with an open hand. Only the secure can wash feet, touch lepers, and give extravagantly.

One of the most impactful and transformative shifts you can make as a believer is to get your mind and heart around this simple, but powerful truth...

In Jesus, we are not servants, even though we happily serve. We are beloved sons and daughters. And of us, the Father says today, "You are always with me. And everything I have is yours." Oh, what a wonderful gift is this thing called grace.

CONCLUSION

YES, IT'S GRACE... PERIOD.

At the very end of his gospel, the apostle John made the following observation:

> And there are also many other things that Jesus did, which if they were written one by one, I suppose that even the world itself could not contain the books that would be written. Amen. (John 21:25)

Here at the end of our exploration of God's grace, I could say something very similar. There simply is not enough paper in the world to contain the books that could be written unveiling the wonders of God's amazing grace. Of course an infinite God would exhibit infinitely intricate dimensions of generosity.

On the opening pages I warned you, "At times you may be tempted to argue with the words on the page. You may want to shout, 'That can't possibly be right! That sounds too good to be true!'" Was I right? I have a friend who likes to say, "If you're explaining the gospel to a lost person and their first response isn't

'That sounds too good to be true,' then you're telling it wrong." And yet if you're like most believers, the truths I've put forward here rang a bell in your deepest heart. Something inside of you said, "Yes! *This* is the God who saved me. *This* is the way of the One who designed our gorgeous world and hung millions of galaxies in place, yet takes notice when common sparrows fall to the ground. *This* is the truth. *This is good news.*"

I suspect that if you've stuck with me thus far, a lot of your questions have been answered and many of your initial objections have been addressed. But in closing, perhaps I should tackle what is, in my experience, the most common objection to fully embracing the full implications of biblical grace. And believe me, there are objections.

Some will react with alarm to the truths I've laid out on these pages. They'll talk about "oars and rowing" and conditions and "what abouts" and "greasy grace." They'll mean well. They'll be sincere. They'll be good people who love our Lord. But I believe with all my heart they'll be mistaken. As I illustrated in the "Start Here" opening of this book, many people simply don't know how to receive a gift. The truth is, for some it really does seem impossible that God could be *that* generous. Or that His offer of eternal relationship and connection could require nothing more than being humble enough to say yes to it. Or that we continue our lives in God the same way we began them. That is, "by grace through faith...and even that faith is not of ourselves...it's not of works, so none of us can boast or brag" (see Ephesians 2:8–9).

For others, however, it's fear that keeps them from embracing what now seems so obvious to me. "Fear of *what*?" you may be wondering. The answer is fear of *themselves*. Fear of what they might start doing—or stop doing—if they actually believed they didn't have anything to contribute to the maintenance of their salvation. Fear that, without the need to earn, or merit, or deserve the blessings of sonship, they might just go off the rails. Fear that living this life requires a white-knuckled grip on the oars of good works and good behavior. Fear that if they stopped being afraid of their Father, they might just go wild.

In a sense, many believers are afraid to stop being afraid.

When that's the case, they invariably are also afraid for other believers to stop being afraid—especially those they care about. When you sincerely love someone, you want the best for them. And if you're convinced that embracing the full implications of grace as I've laid them out here will cause Christians to start living like pagans on spring break, you don't want them to embrace it.

Which is why many well-intentioned pastors get nervous when someone preaches the g-word to their congregations without heaping portions of *but*s and *however*s and *on the other hand*s and *two oars* and other disclaimers to water down the stunning implications of the new covenant.

Andrew Owen is the pastor of an amazing church in Glasgow, Scotland. Not only is Destiny Church extremely large by UK standards, Andrew oversees more than fourteen hundred churches his congregation has planted around the world. Andrew is also a friend of Gateway Church, the church I founded and have been privileged to pastor for more than two decades. He comes to mind right now because of a story he tells in the introduction to his book *Astronomical Grace: The Greatest Story Never Told.*[9]

There, Pastor Owen describes a time he was invited to speak to a large church somewhere in England. The church had multiple, back-to-back services on Sunday morning, and Andrew was scheduled to preach at all of them. His planned message topic? "Grace and the finished work of Jesus Christ." In the first service he described an invitation to relationship with God that didn't hinge on our own efforts, our own works, and our own righteousness. One that instead was built entirely on Jesus' perfect and complete fulfillment of everything the Law required. At the end of the message, dozens came forward to give their lives to Jesus and hundreds of others, having received a glimpse of the goodness and kindness of God, came forward for prayer.

After the service, Andrew was approached by the pastor of the church and told he wouldn't be preaching in the remaining services. The pastor and the leadership team said they were shocked by the content of his message and would not allow it to be preached again in their church. When he asked why, the answer was that it was "too dangerous."

What was the danger they perceived? It is often phrased this way: The message of grace will be taken as license to sin.

I know this objection well. In the past, well-intentioned people have told me, "Robert, you'd better not preach on grace too much because if you do, your people will just go out and sin."

My response is usually twofold. First of all, they're not *my* people. They're Jesus' people and I'm just shepherding and stewarding one of the Good Shepherd's many flocks. Second, as kindly and tactfully as possible, I say, "You don't know what you're talking about. Grace does not produce sin. Grace produces righteousness." Please let me explain.

> In the past, well-intentioned people have told me, "Robert, you'd better not preach on grace too much because if you do, your people will just go out and sin."

You may have noticed how so many spiritual truths appear to be a paradox. That means they're the opposite of what our natural minds expect to be true. Examples?

- Jesus said the path to be the greatest in any group is to be the servant of all (see Matthew 23:11).
- Those who wish to save their lives must lose their lives (see John 12:25).
- Supernatural strength comes from recognizing our weakness (see 2 Corinthians 12:10).
- There is one who hoards yet decreases. While there is one who gives away, yet experiences increase! (see Proverbs 11:24).
- Only in surrendering our wills to Jesus do we find real freedom (see John 8:31–36).

I could cite others, but you get the point. In a similar way the Law and grace also present a paradox. Those who submit themselves to the strict constraints and harsh penalties of the Law only find themselves sinning more. Sin uses the Law to stir up the flesh's desire to sin more. (So says Romans 7:7–8.) But those who enter the liberty of grace live more and more righteously. The deeper the revelation of grace sinks into their minds and gets rooted into their identities, the more their desires, thoughts, habits, and actions come into alignment with who they truly are in Jesus. Nevertheless, our natural minds struggle to grasp this. Like so many other spiritual truths, it's totally counterintuitive.

So how does this work? How is it that the holy Law can't produce holiness, yet grace does? The spiritual dynamics of this are evident in our Bibles.

Firstly, the Law is built on fear while grace is built on love. Love does what fear can never do. It's the strongest force for change and transformation in the universe.

> Love does what fear can never do. It's the strongest force for change and transformation in the universe.

God is love (see 1 John 4:8). God's love drew us and saved us (see 1 John 4:9–10, 19; Ephesians 1:4–5). In love, Jesus is washing us, His Bride, with the water of the Word—something husbands are encouraged to emulate (see Ephesians 5:25–26). Love drives out fear, particularly the fear of punishment (see 1 John 4:18). "Speaking the truth *in love*" (Ephesians 4:15, emphasis added) is what will cause the Church to mature and accurately present a full and complete image of Jesus to the world.

So what about the Law? The Law, as a reflection of God's perfection and holiness, is itself perfect. Yet its power actually pulls us in the other direction. The Law excites our fleshly desires (see Romans 7:5–8). The Law ministers condemnation (see 2 Corinthians 3:9). The Law ministers death (see 2 Corinthians 3:7). The God-assigned job of the Law was to make it clear that we are all helpless sinners in desperate need of grace (see Romans 3:19–20). And it's really good at its job! This is only the first biblical reason why grace, properly understood, doesn't create a license to sin. Here's the second one.

Connection to God—His presence—is the surest, highest source of transformation. Nothing causes the desires, ways, and habits of your old, dead self to fall away like simply sitting in your heavenly Father's presence. God has glory, and glory changes us:

> But we all, with unveiled face, beholding as in a mirror the glory of the Lord, *are being transformed* into the same image

from glory to glory, just as by the Spirit of the Lord. (2 Corinthians 3:18, emphasis added)

Yes, communion—intimate, ongoing fellowship—with our wonderful Father changes us. It can't help but do so. So ask yourself: Which makes you more likely to run to, and spend extended time with, God...the Law with its ministry of condemnation?... Or the truth about grace?

The good news of grace—the understanding that you're never coming to God in your righteousness but rather in Jesus' righteousness—removes all hesitation to run to your Father's arms at any moment. When you get a revelation of grace you come gladly, expectantly, boldly, and confidently to the Father and enjoy your time with Him. There, in the light of His love, you'll become aware of areas of your thinking or doing that aren't in alignment with who you really are in Christ. And there in His fatherly hands you'll be shaped and molded. "Conformed to the image of His Son," as Romans 8:29 tells us. We read in Philippians 2:13, "For it is God who works in you both to will and to do for His good pleasure." This is grace at work in you. When you stand in that grace you can be confident "that He who has begun a good work in you will complete it until the day of Jesus Christ" (Philippians 1:6).

In contrast, as long as you have one foot in the Law, you will invariably be reluctant to go to Him. Oh sure, when your circumstances get really desperate, you'll approach Him, but only by slinking in on your belly, filled with condemnation, and feeling utterly disqualified. You'll expect nothing so you'll likely come away with nothing. And you won't stay long.

> Connection is the only way to transformation.

Connection is the only way to

transformation. I'm talking about connection to God through our Savior, Jesus. You cannot *will* yourself into being a fruitful Christian who lives righteously. There is simply not enough willpower and self-discipline in the world. Using willpower and self-discipline requires you to keep your eyes focused on yourself. Your flesh. Your behavior. And guess what the Word says about that:

> For those who are in accord with the flesh set their minds on the things of the flesh, but those who are in accord with the Spirit, the things of the Spirit. For *the mind set on the flesh is death*, but the mind set on the Spirit is life and peace, because *the mind set on the flesh is hostile toward God*; for it does not subject itself to the law of God, for it is not even able to do so, and those who are in the flesh cannot please God. (Romans 8:5–8 NASB, emphasis added)

Being sin-conscious will produce more sin in you. Being righteousness-conscious will result in more righteous behavior. And only renewing your mind to the truth about grace can make you righteousness-conscious.

Being sin-conscious will produce more sin in you. Being righteousness-conscious will result in more righteous behavior.

How many of us were taught that we ought to have a daily quiet time with God? Approaching this "ought" with a servant's mindset made it a duty to perform. A task box to be checked off so we could hopefully feel like we'd earned some credits with the God who was continually disappointed in us. We were taught we needed to spend time with God even though the servant's mindset convinced us that God was almost certainly mad at us. How eager are you to enter the boss's office when you think you've messed up and he's angry about it? The servant mindset drains every drop of joy from fellowship with God.

But those with the mindset of a daughter or son don't view fellowship with their Father as an *obligation*. They view it as an *opportunity*. They understand the kind of covenant they're in (a parity covenant between God the Father and God the Son). Therefore, they see the door to God's office as wide open to them all the time. They (correctly) anticipate their Father is in a good mood and will be delighted to see them. Why? Because they know their status with Him is not based on their performance. It is wholly rooted in Jesus' perfect performance. They know they are in Christ and He is in them. They come clothed in a robe of righteousness and wearing His ring of authority, and they know it. Yes, only the truth about grace fosters an intimate, ongoing, life-connection to God. And only that connection can make possible the kind of transformation that produces righteous living.

> Those with the mindset of a daughter or son don't view fellowship with their Father as an *obligation*. They view it as an *opportunity*.

We can't talk about transformation of the believer without mentioning Romans 12:2. It's one of the most familiar and frequently quoted verses about transformation in the Bible:

And do not be conformed to this world, but *be transformed by the renewing of your mind*, that you may prove what is that good and acceptable and perfect will of God. (emphasis added)

How many times have you read or heard that "renewing your mind" produces the transformation that keeps you from being "conformed to this world"? It's absolutely true! But you need to ask, "Renewing my mind to *what* exactly?" The answer is: renewing your mind to what Paul just revealed in the previous eleven chapters! And as we've seen repeatedly on these pages, those first eleven chapters of Romans reveal Paul making a detailed, elaborate case that we are no longer under Law, but rather under grace. He says so explicitly in Romans 6:14: "For sin shall not have dominion over you, *for you are not under law but under grace*" (emphasis added). The renewing of your mind to that reality will cause you to be transformed.

Paul must have heard the license-to-sin argument whenever he taught the truth about God's amazing grace. He anticipates this very objection, and answers it, right in the middle of explaining grace in Romans!

> So what do we do, then? *Do we persist in sin so that God's kindness and grace will increase?* What a terrible thought! We have died to sin once and for all, as a dead man passes away from this life. So how could we live under sin's rule a moment longer? Or have you forgotten that all of us who were immersed into union with Jesus, the Anointed One, were immersed into union with his death? (Romans 6:1–3 TPT, emphasis added)

This isn't the only passage where Paul anticipated and addressed the license-to-sin objection. It seems there is nothing new about the fear that caused those pastors to stop Andrew Owen from preaching grace again.

Do you want to be a more fruitful believer? Then, again, the free, uninhibited communion with the Father and abiding in the Son that a revelation of grace produces in you is the path you want to take. Remember, Jesus is the vine, and only by abiding in Him is it even possible to bear fruit. "Apart from Me you can do nothing," Jesus told us (John 15:5 NASB).

Are you beginning to see it? Shame, condemnation, feeling disqualified, and just generally having the mindset of a servant rather than a son keeps you away from intimate fellowship with the Father. It keeps you from abiding in the Vine. And as I said above, *connection* is the only way to transformation. When you live in the daily, intimate communion and friendship that the gift of sonship makes possible, it changes your "wanter." You progressively, incrementally start wanting what your Father wants rather than what the old, dead-and-buried version of you wanted. No, grace isn't a license to sin. It's the only pathway to a fruit-bearing lifestyle that is ever-increasingly free from sin.

Seeing Jesus as the Vine should make us mindful of the Tree of Life described in Genesis. Adam and Eve were meant to eat of the Tree of Life. We know this because God said, "Of *every tree* of the garden you may freely eat; but of the tree of the knowledge of good and evil you shall not eat..." (Genesis 2:16–17, emphasis added). We also know our common ancestors ended up at the *wrong tree*.

Here's the thing. Many believers today are *living* at the wrong tree. The scribes and the Pharisees knew the Old Testament Scriptures exhaustively. They studied them obsessively. But they were reading the Bible at the wrong tree. They read it like a rule book rather than as a revelation of God's redemptive love for the world. Which is why they failed to recognize the Messiah, the Redeemer of the world, when He was standing right in front of them. Instead of recognizing Him, they relentlessly pointed out all the ways He and His followers were violating the rules (as they perceived them).

We, too, can read the Bible at the wrong tree. And when we do, we, like the scribes and Pharisees, fail to recognize what the Redeemer has done for us and wants to do through us. We struggle and strive to change from the outside in. And we fail, over and over and over again.

The "Tree of Life" is the presence of God. The Fall resulted in a barrier that blocked our access to Him and His life. But by grace, Jesus, by hanging on a tree, opened the way back to Him. When we read our Bibles in the light of that tree, we experience life and freedom and joy. And we are changed...from the inside out.

> Many believers today are *living* at the wrong tree.

> Read your Bible in the light of the Tree of Life and you'll discover the message of God's grace woven throughout.

Read your Bible in the light of the Tree of Life and you'll discover the message of God's grace woven throughout. It's practically on every page if only you have eyes to see it (and I believe you now do!). It's there in the opening chapters of Genesis when a loving God comes searching for a couple who have disobeyed him and in doing so unleashed incalculable misery on their descendants and the planet those descendants will call home. It's there:

- In His tender crafting of garments, undeserved gifts designed to cover their naked exposure and shame.
- In His putting Abraham to sleep while a substitute, a proxy, walked between the sacrificed animal halves.

- In the sudden appearance of a ram caught in a thicket just when Abraham desperately needed a "substitute" sacrifice.
- In the choosing of Jacob, the second-born son, as the one who would become the founder of the nation of Israel. And in the changing of his name from one that means "supplanter" or "usurper" to one that means "He retains God."
- In Jacob's gift to Joseph of a special long robe signifying favor, even though Joseph was the youngest son at that time.
- In the details of the Israelites' first Passover, where the blood of a perfect, spotless lamb on the doorposts of a household extended the gift of life.
- In the details of the Day of Atonement ritual (Yom Kippur), where the priest inspected the *sacrifice* for faults, not the *person* who brought the sacrifice.
- In God's instructions to the prophet Hosea, to take as his wife a deeply immoral woman, and to take her back after she left him and was profoundly unfaithful.

Grace is in the parables of Jesus. And it saturates the writings of Paul who, by the way, did not learn the truth of the gospel second-hand. He received it directly from Jesus by divine revelation and visitation (see Galatians 1:12).

It was to make possible a lifestyle of freedom that Jesus set you free. There remains therefore a Sabbath rest for you and me. One in which we have ceased from our laborious striving to earn or merit or deserve our place at the Father's table.

Just as there were *two* trees in the garden, and just as the father in Jesus' parable had *two* sons . . . there are *two* options for living the Christian life. One creates a life of struggle, sweat, failure, condemnation, shame, and distance from God. The other creates a life of freedom, faith, fruitfulness, and fellowship with a loving Father.

The first could be characterized as "Grace Plus…" or "Grace And…" or "Grace But…" The second is the one I recommend to you with all my heart. It is…

Grace. Period.

NOTES

1. Charles Spurgeon, "The Death of Christ for His People," https://www.the kingdomcollective.com/spurgeon/sermon/2656.

2. James Strong, *Strong's Exhaustive Concordance of the Bible*, updated edition (Hendrickson Academic, 2009).

3. James A. Swanson, *A Dictionary of Biblical Languages: Greek*, second edition (Logos Research Systems, electronic/digital, 2001).

4. James Swanson, *A Dictionary of Biblical Languages: Greek; New Testament* (Logos Research Systems, electronic/digital, 1997).

5. John Sheasby with Ken Gire, *The Birthright: Out of the Servants' Quarters into the Father's House* (Zondervan, 2010), p. 99.

6. Dudley Hall, *Orphans No More: Learning to Live Loved* (Kerygma Ventures Press, 2011), p. 13.

7. Kris Vallaton, *The Supernatural Ways of Royalty* (Destiny Image Publishers, 2006).

8. David Holland, *Praying Grace: 55 Meditations and Declarations on the Finished Work of Christ* (Broadstreet Publishing, 2020), p. 90.

9. Andrew Owen, *Astronomical Grace: The Greatest Story Never Told* (Breakfast for Seven Publishing, 2022).

ADDITIONAL CREDITS

ABOUT THE AUTHOR

ROBERT MORRIS is the senior pastor of Gateway Church, a multi-campus church based in the Dallas–Fort Worth metroplex. Since it began in 2000, the church has grown to more than 100,000 active attendees. His television program airs in over 190 countries, and his radio program, *Worship & the Word with Pastor Robert*, airs in more than 6,800 cities. He serves as chancellor of The King's University and is the bestselling author of numerous books, including *The Blessed Life*, *Frequency*, *Beyond Blessed*, and *Take the Day Off*. Robert and his wife, Debbie, have been married forty-three years and are blessed with one married daughter, two married sons, and nine grandchildren.